D1500238

PARTICIPATION AND DEMOCRATIC THEORY

PARTICIPATION AND DEMOCRATIC THEORY

CAROLE PATEMAN

*Mary Ewart Research Fellow, Somerville College,
Oxford*

CAMBRIDGE

AT THE UNIVERSITY PRESS

1970

Published by the Syndics of the Cambridge University Press
Bentley House, 200 Euston Road, London NW1 2DB
American Branch: 32 East 57th Street, New York, N.Y. 10022

© Cambridge University Press 1970

Library of Congress Catalogue Card Number: 71-120193

ISBN 0 521 07856 3

First published 1970
Reprinted 1972

First printed in Great Britain by Alden & Mowbray Ltd at the Alden Press, Oxford
Reprinted in Great Britain by
Redwood Press Limited, Trowbridge & London

CONTENTS

CHAPTER I

Recent theories of democracy
and the 'classical myth'

During the last few years of the 1960s the word 'participation' became part of the popular political vocabulary. This took place under the impetus of demands, notably from students, for new areas of participation to be opened up—in this case in the sphere of higher education—and of demands by various groups for the practical implementation of rights of participation that were theirs in theory. In France 'participation' was one of the last of De Gaulle's rallying calls; in Britain we have seen the idea given official blessing in the Skeffington Report on planning, and in America the anti-poverty programme included a provision for the 'maximum feasible participation' of those concerned. The widespread use of the term in the mass media has tended to mean that any precise, meaningful content has almost disappeared; 'participation' is used to refer to a wide variety of different situations by different people. The popularity of the concept provides a good reason for devoting some attention to it, but more importantly, the recent upsurge of demands for more participation raises a central question of political theory; the place of 'participation' in a modern, viable theory of democracy.

It is rather ironical that the idea of participation should have become so popular, particularly with students, for among political theorists and political sociologists the widely accepted theory of democracy (so widely accepted that one might call it the orthodox doctrine) is one in which the concept of participation has only the most minimal role. Indeed, not only has it a minimal role but a prominent feature of recent theories of democracy is the emphasis placed on the dangers inherent in wide popular participation in politics. These characteristics derive from two major concerns of recent, particularly American, writers on democratic theory. First, their conviction that the theories of earlier writers on democracy (the so-called 'classical theorists') which have the idea of the maximum participation of all the people at their heart, are in need of drastic revision, if not outright rejection. Secondly, a preoccupation with the stability of the political system, and with the conditions, or prerequisites, necessary to ensure that stability; this preoccupation has its origins in the contrast drawn between 'democracy' and 'totalitarianism' as the only two political alternatives available in the modern world.

It is not difficult to see how recent democratic theory has come to rest on this basis; without too great an over-simplification it can be said to result from one intellectual event of this century, the development of political sociology, and from one historical event, the rise of totalitarian states.

At the beginning of the century the size and complexity of industrialized societies and the emergence of bureaucratic forms of organisation seemed to many empirically minded writers on politics to cast grave doubts on the possibility of the attainment of democracy as that concept was usually understood. Mosca and Michels were two of the best known and most influential writers to advance such a thesis. The former argued that in every society an élite must rule and, in his later writings, combined this élite theory with an argument for representative institutions. Michels with his famous 'iron law of oligarchy'—formulated on the basis of an investigation of German Social Democratic parties that were ostensibly dedicated to the principles of democracy inside their own ranks—appeared to show that we were faced with a choice; either organisation, which in the twentieth century seemed indispensable, or democracy, but not both. Thus, although democracy as the rule of the people by means of the maximum participation of all the people might still be an ideal, grave doubts, doubts put forward in the name of social science, appeared to have been cast upon the possibility of realising this ideal.

But by the middle of the century even the ideal itself seemed to many to have been called in question; at least, 'democracy' was still the ideal, but it was the emphasis on participation that had become suspect and with it the 'classical' formulation of democratic theory. The collapse of the Weimar Republic, with its high rates of mass participation, into fascism, and the post-war establishment of totalitarian regimes based on mass participation, albeit participation backed by intimidation and coercion, underlay the tendency for 'participation' to become linked to the concept of totalitarianism rather than that of democracy. The spectre of totalitarianism also helps explain the concern with the necessary conditions for stability in a democratic polity, and a further factor here was the instability of so many states in the post-war world, especially ex-colonial states that rarely maintained a democratic political system on Western lines.

If this background had led to great doubts and reservations about earlier theories of democracy, then the facts revealed by the post-war expansion of political sociology appear to have convinced most recent writers that these doubts were fully justified. Data from large-scale empirical investigations into political attitudes and behaviour, undertaken in most Western countries over the past twenty or thirty years, have revealed that the outstanding characteristic of most citizens, more especially those in the lower socio-economic status (SES) groups, is a general lack of interest in politics and political activity and further, that widespread non-democratic or authoritarian attitudes exist, again particularly among lower socio-economic status groups. The conclusion drawn (often by political sociologists wearing political theorists' hats) is that the 'classical' picture of democratic man is hopelessly unrealistic, and moreover, that in view of the facts about political attitudes, an increase in political participation by present non-participants could upset the stability of the democratic system.

There was a further factor that helped along the process of the rejection of earlier democratic theories, and that was the now familiar argument that those theories were normative and 'value-laden', whereas modern political theory should be scientific and empirical, grounded firmly in the facts of political life. But even so, it may be doubted whether the revision of democratic theory would have been undertaken with such enthusiasm by so many writers if it had not been that this very question of the apparent contrast between the facts of political life and attitudes and their characterisation in earlier theories had not already been taken up, and answered, by Joseph Schumpeter. His extraordinarily influential book *Capitalism, Socialism and Democracy* (1943) was in fact written before the vast amounts of empirical information that we now have on politics became available, but nevertheless Schumpeter considered that the facts showed that 'classical' democratic theory was in need of revision, and he provided just such a revised theory. More than that, however, and even more importantly for the theories that followed, he put forward a new, realistic *definition* of democracy. An understanding of the nature of Schumpeter's theory is vital for an appreciation of more recent work in democratic theory for it is elaborated within the framework established by Schumpeter and based on his definition of democracy.

The starting point of Schumpeter's analysis is an attack on the notion of democratic theory as a theory of means and ends; democracy he asserts is a theory unassociated with any particular ideals or ends. 'Democracy is a political *method*, that is to say, a certain type of institutional arrangement for arriving at political—legislative and administrative—decisions.' In so far as one expressed 'uncompromising allegiance' to democracy this was because one expected the method to further other ideals, for example justice.[1]

---

[1] Schumpeter (1943, p. 242) (Schumpeter's emphasis). To convince his readers of the

The procedure that Schumpeter followed in formulating his theory of democracy was to set up a model of what he called the 'classical doctrine' of democracy, to examine the deficiencies of this model and then to offer an alternative. (This model and Schumpeter's criticisms of it will be considered later.) Schumpeter thought that 'most students of politics' would agree with his criticisms and would also agree with his revised theory of democracy which 'is much truer to life and at the same time salvages much of what sponsors of the democratic method really mean by this term' (p. 269). As Schumpeter's main criticism of the 'classical doctrine' was that the central participatory and decision making role of the people rested on empirically unrealistic foundations, in his revised theory it is the competition by potential decision makers for the people's vote that is the vital feature. Thus, Schumpeter offered the following as a modern, realistic definition of the democratic method: 'That institutional arrangement for arriving at political decisions in which individuals acquire the power to decide by means of a competitive struggle for the people's vote' (p. 269). On this definition it is the competition for leadership that is the distinctive feature of democracy, and the one which allows us to distinguish the democratic from other political methods. By this method everyone is, in principle, free to compete for leadership in free elections so that the usual civil liberties are necessary.[1] Schumpeter compared the political competition for votes to the operation of the (economic) market; voters like consumers choose between the policies (products) offered by competing political entrepreneurs and the parties regulate the competition like trade associations in the economic sphere.

Schumpeter paid some attention to the necessary conditions for the operation of the democratic method. Apart from civil liberties, tolerance of others' opinions and a 'national character and national habits of a certain type' were required, and the operation of the democratic method itself could not be relied upon to produce these. Another requirement was for 'all the interests that matter' to be virtually unanimous in their allegiance to the 'structural principles of existing society' (pp. 295–6). Schumpeter

validity of this argument, Schumpeter proposed a 'mental experiment'. Imagine a country which, democratically, persecuted Jews, witches and Christians; we should not approve of these practices just because they had been decided upon according to the democratic method, therefore, democracy cannot be an end. But as Bachrach points out, such systematic persecution would conflict with the rules of procedure necessary if the country's political method is to be called 'democratic' (Bachrach, 1967, pp. 18–20). Nor does Schumpeter make it clear exactly why we should expect *this* political method to lead to e.g. justice.

[1] Despite the freedom in principle, Schumpeter thought that in fact a political or ruling class was necessary to provide candidates for leadership (p. 291).

did not, however, regard universal suffrage as necessary; he thought that property, race or religious qualifications were all perfectly compatible with the democratic method.[1]

The only means of participation open to the citizen in Schumpeter's theory are voting for leaders and discussion. He rules out such usually acceptable activity as 'bombarding' representatives with letters as against the spirit of the democratic method because, he argues, it is in effect an attempt by citizens to control their representatives and this is a negation of the whole concept of leadership. The electorate do not 'normally' control their leaders except by replacing them at elections with alternative leaders, so, 'it seems well to reduce our ideas about this control in the way indicated by our definition' (p. 272). In Schumpeter's theory of democracy, participation has no special or central role. All that is entailed is that enough citizens participate to keep the electoral machinery—the institutional arrangements—working satisfactorily. The focus of the theory is on the minority of leaders. 'The electoral mass', says Schumpeter, 'is incapable of action other than a stampede' (p. 283), so that it is leaders who must be active, initiate and decide, and it is competition between leaders for votes that is the characteristically democratic element in this political method.

There is no doubt about the importance of Schumpeter's theory for later theories of democracy. His notion of a 'classical theory', his characterisation of the 'democratic method' and the role of participation in that method have all become almost universally accepted in recent writing on democratic theory. One of the few places where more recent theorists differ slightly from Schumpeter is over the question of whether a basic 'democratic character' is necessary for democracy and whether the existence of that character depends on the working of the democratic method. We shall now consider four well-known examples of recent work on democratic theory; those of Berelson, Dahl, Sartori and Eckstein. There is more emphasis on the stability of the political system in these works than in Schumpeter, but the theory of democracy common to them all is one descended directly from Schumpeter's attack on the 'classical' theory of democracy.

In Chapter 14 of *Voting* (1954), which is called 'Democratic Theory and Democratic Practice', Berelson's theoretical orientation, a functionalist one, is very different from that of Schumpeter, but he has the same aim.[2] He sets out to examine the implications for 'classical' democratic theory of a

---

[1] (pp. 244–5). Here more recent theories do not follow him.
See also Berelson (1952). For some criticisms of the functionalist aspects of Berelson's theory see Duncan and Lukes (1963).

'confrontation' with the empirical evidence to be found in the previous chapters of the book. For the purpose of this confrontation he adopts Schumpeter's strategy of presenting a model of the 'classical theory'—or, more accurately, a model of the qualities and attitudes that this theory is asserted to require on the part of individual citizens—and this procedure reveals that 'certain requirements commonly assumed for the successful operation of democracy are not met by the behaviour of the "average citizen"'.[1] For example, 'the democratic citizen is expected to be interested and to participate in political affairs' but 'in Elmira the majority of the people vote but in general they do not give evidence of sustained interest' (1954, p. 307). Nevertheless, despite this and all the other deficiencies in democratic practice, Western democracies have survived; so we are faced with a paradox,

Individual voters today seem unable to satisfy the requirements for a democratic system of government outlined by political theorists. But the *system of democracy* does meet certain requirements for a going political organisation. The individual members may not meet all the standards, but the whole nevertheless survives and grows (p. 312, Berelson's italics).

The statement of this paradox enables us to see, according to Berelson, the mistake made by the 'classical' writers, and to see why their theory does not give us an accurate picture of the working of existing democratic political systems. 'Classical' theory, he argues, concentrated on the individual citizen, virtually ignoring the political system itself, and where it did deal with the latter, it considered specific institutions and not those 'general features necessary if the institutions are to work as required'. Berelson lists the conditions necessary 'if political democracy is to survive' as follows: intensity of conflict must be limited, the rate of change restrained, social and economic stability maintained, and a pluralist social organisation and basic consensus must exist.[2]

According to Berelson, the earlier theorists also assumed that a politically homogeneous citizenry was required in a democracy (homogeneous that

[1] Berelson (1954, p. 307), Berelson, in common with almost all other writers who talk of 'classical' democratic theory, does not say from *which* writers his model is drawn. In the earlier article he remarks of the composite set of attitudes he draws up, that 'while not all of them may be required in any single political theory of democracy, all of them are mentioned in one or another theory' (1952, p. 314). But, again, no names are given.

[2] (1954, pp. 312–13). The specific connection between these conditions and democracy is not made clear; the first three would seem to be required, almost tautologically, for *any* political system to continue. Berelson adds that he is going to continue by exploring 'the values' of the political system. In fact what he does it to look at the 'requirements of the system'; see the section heading on p. 313.

is in attitudes and behaviour). In fact what is required, and happily, what is found, is heterogeneity. This heterogeneity is necessary because we expect our political system to perform 'contradictory functions' but, despite this, the system works: it works because of the way in which qualities and attitudes are distributed among the electorate; this distribution enables the contradictions to be resolved while the stability of the system is also maintained. Thus the system is both stable and flexible, for example, because political traditions in families and ethnic groups and the long-lasting nature of political loyalties contribute to stability, whereas, 'the voters least admirable when measured against individual requirements contribute most when measured against the aggregate requirement for flexibility . . . they may be the least partisan and the least interested voters, but they perform a valuable function for the entire system'.[1]

In short, limited participation and apathy have a positive function for the whole system by cushioning the shock of disagreement, adjustment and change.

Berelson concludes by arguing that his theory is not only realistic and descriptively accurate but that it also includes the values that 'classical' theory ascribed to individuals. He says that the existing distribution of attitudes among the electorate 'can perform the functions and incorporate the same values ascribed by some theorists to each individual in the system as well as to the constitutive political institutions'! This being so we should not, therefore, reject the normative content of the older theory— that is presumably the account of attitudes required by individual citizens —but this content should be revised to fit in with present realities.[2]

Berelson's theory provides us with a clear statement of some of the main arguments of recent work in democratic theory. For example, the argument that a modern theory of democracy must be descriptive in form and focus on the on-going political system. From this standpoint we can see that high levels of participation and interest are required from a minority of citizens only and, moreover, the apathy and disinterest of the majority play a valuable role in maintaining the stability of the system as a whole. Thus we arrive at the argument that the amount of participation that actually obtains is just about the amount that is required for a stable system of democracy.

[1] (1954, p. 316). It is difficult to see why Berelson calls the items he cites 'contradictory'. Certainly they might be empirically difficult to obtain at the same time, but it is possible to have, and not illogical to ask for, both stability and flexibility or to have voters who express free, self-determined choices, at the same time making use of the best information and guidance from leaders (see pp. 313–14).

[2] (1954, pp. 322–3). The exclamation mark is well placed in the passage quoted, which verges on the nonsensical.

Berelson does not explicitly consider what characteristics are required for a political system to be described as 'democratic', given that maximum participation by all citizens is not one of them. An answer to this question can be found in two studies by Dahl, *A Preface to Democratic Theory* (1956) and *Hierarchy, Democracy and Bargaining in Politics and Economics* (1956a), and it is an answer that closely follows Schumpeter's definition.

Dahl does not 'confront' theory and fact in the same way as Berelson; indeed, Dahl seems very uncertain about whether there is, or is not, such a thing as the 'classical theory of democracy'. At the beginning of *A Preface to Democratic Theory* he remarks that 'there is no democratic theory—there are only democratic theories'.[1] In the earlier paper, however, he had written that 'classical theory is demonstrably invalid in some respects' (1965a, p. 86). Certainly Dahl regards the theories that he criticises in *A Preface to Democratic Theory* (the 'Madisonian' and the 'Populist') as inadequate for the present day and his theory of democracy as polyarchy—the rule of multiple minorities—is presented as a more adequate replacement for these, as an explanatory, modern theory of democracy.

Dahl offers a list of the defining characteristics of a democracy and these, following Schumpeter's argument that democracy is a political method, are a list of 'institutional arrangements' that centre on the electoral process (1956, p. 84). Elections are central to the democratic method because they provide the mechanism through which the control of leaders by non-leaders can take place; 'democratic theory is concerned with the processes by which ordinary citizens exert a relatively high degree of control over leaders' (p. 3). Dahl, like Schumpeter, emphasises that more should not be put into the notion of 'control' than is realistically warranted. He points out that contemporary political writings emphasise that the democratic relationship is only one of a number of social control techniques that in fact co-exist in modern democratic polities and this diversity must be taken account of in a modern theory of democracy (1956a, p. 83). Nor is it any use putting forward a theory that requires maximum participation from ordinary people for 'control' to take place when we know that most tend to be disinterested and apathetic about politics, and Dahl puts forward the hypothesis that a relatively small proportion of individuals in any form of social organisation will take up decision-making opportunities.[2] It is, therefore, on the other side of the electoral process, on the competition between leaders for the votes of the people, that 'control' depends; the fact that the individual can switch his support from

[1] (1956, p. 1). But he also refers at least once to 'traditional theory' (p. 131). However, cf. Dahl (1966) where he says there never was a classical theory of democracy.
[2] (1956a, p. 87). See also (1956, pp. 81 and 138).

one set of leaders to another ensures that leaders are 'relatively responsive' to non-leaders. It is this competition that is the specifically democratic element in the method, and the value of a democratic (polyarchical) system over other political methods lies in the fact that it makes possible an extension of the number, size and diversity of the minorities that can bring their influence to bear on policy decisions, and on the whole political ethos of the society (1956, pp. 133–4).

The theory of polyarchy may also give us 'a satisfactory theory about political equality' (1956, p. 84). Once again we must not ignore political realities. Political equality must not be defined as equality of political control or power for, as Dahl notes, the lower socio-economic status groups, the majority, are 'triply barred' from such equality by their relatively greater inactivity, their limited access to resources, and—in the United States—by 'Madison's nicely contrived system of constitutional checks' (1956, p. 81). In a modern theory of democracy 'political equality' refers to the existence of universal suffrage (one man, one vote) with its sanction through the electoral competition for votes and, more importantly, to the fact of equality of opportunity of access to influence over decision makers through inter-electoral processes by which different groups in the electorate make their demands heard. Officials not only listen to the various groups, but 'expect to suffer in some significant way if they do not placate the group, its leaders or its most vociferous members' (p. 145).

Another aspect of Dahl's theory that is of particular interest is his discussion of the social prerequisites for a polyarchical system. A basic prerequisite is a consensus on norms, at least among leaders. (The necessary and sufficient, institutional conditions for polyarchy can be formulated as norms (1956, pp. 75–6).) This consensus depends on 'social training' which, in turn, depends on the existing amount of agreement on policy choices and norms, so that an increase or decrease in one element will affect the others (p. 77). The social training takes place through the family, schools, churches, newspapers, etc., and Dahl distinguishes three kinds of training: reinforcing, neutral and negative. He argues that 'it is reasonable to suppose that these three kinds of training operate on members of most, if not all, polyarchical organisations and perhaps on members of many hierarchical organisations as well' (1956, p. 76). Dahl does not say what the training consists of, nor does he offer any suggestions as to which kind of training is likely to be produced by which kind of control system, but he does remark that its efficacy will depend on the existing, 'deepest predispositions of the individual' (p. 82). Presumably, 'effective' social training would be a training which would develop individual attitudes that support the democratic norms; on the other hand, Dahl argues that no single 'democratic character' is required, as suggested by earlier theorists, because this is unrealistic in the face of the 'blatant fact' that individuals are members of diverse kinds of social control systems. What is required is personalities that can adapt to different kinds of roles in different control systems (1956a, p. 89), but Dahl gives no indication how training to produce this kind of personality aids the consensus on *democratic* norms.

Finally, Dahl puts forward an argument about the possible dangers inherent in an increase in participation on the part of the ordinary man. Political activity is a prerequisite of polyarchy, but the relationship is an extremely complex one. The lower socio-economic groups are the least politically active and it is also among this group that 'authoritarian' personalities are most frequently found. Thus, to the extent that a rise in political activity brought this group into the political arena, the consensus on norms might decline and hence polyarchy decline. Therefore, an increase over the existing amount of participation could be dangerous to the stability of the democratic system (1956, App. E).

The third theorist of democracy whose work will be discussed is a European writer, Sartori. His book *Democratic Theory* (1962) contains what is perhaps the most extreme version of the revision of earlier theories of democracy. Basically, his theory is an extension of Dahl's theory of democracy as polyarchy so the details of the argument will not be repeated, but Sartori stresses that in a democracy it is not just minorities that rule but (competing) élites. A noteworthy feature of his theory is the emphasis that Sartori places on the dangers of instability and his related views on the proper relationship between democratic theory (the ideal) and democratic practice. According to Sartori a completely unbridgeable gap has appeared between the 'classical' theory and reality; 'the ingratitude typical of the man of our time and his disillusionment with democracy are the reaction to a promised goal that cannot possibly be reached' (p. 54). However, we must be careful not to misunderstand the proper role of democratic theory even when it has been revised and reinterpreted. Once a democratic system has been established—as in Western countries at present—the democratic ideal must be *minimised*. This ideal is a levelling principle that aggravates rather than provides an answer to the real problem in democracies, that of 'retaining verticality', i.e. the structure of authority and leadership; maximised as an 'absolute demand' the (revised) democratic ideal would lead to the 'bankruptcy' of the system (pp. 65 and 96). Today, democracy does not have to be on its guard as it once did against aristocracy but against mediocrity and the danger that it might destroy its own leaders, replacing them by undemocratic counter-élites (p. 119).

The fear that the active participation of the people in the political process leads straight to totalitarianism colours all Sartori's arguments. The people, he says, must 'react', they do not 'act;' react that is to the initiatives and policies of the competing élites (p. 77). Fortunately, this is what the average citizen does in practice and a point of major interest in Sartori's theory is that he is one of the very rare theorists of democracy who actually poses the question, 'How can we account for the inactivity of the average citizen?' His answer is that we do not have to account for it. Arguments that the apathy might be due to illiteracy, poverty or insufficient information have been shown by events to be false, as has the suggestion that it might be due to lack of practice in democracy, 'we have learned that one does not learn how to vote by voting'. Sartori argues that to try to find an answer to the question is a mistaken endeavour for we can only really understand, and take an active interest in, matters of which we have personal experience, or ideas that we can formulate for ourselves, neither of which is possible for the average person where politics is concerned. We must also accept the facts as they are because trying to change them would endanger the maintenance of the democratic method and, further, he argues that the only way in which we could attempt to change them would be either to coerce the apathetic or to penalise the active minority, neither of which method is acceptable. Sartori concludes that the apathy of the majority is 'nobody's fault in particular, and it is time we stopped seeking scapegoats' (pp. 87–90).

The theories of democracy considered so far have been mainly concerned with showing what sort of a theory is necessary if it is adequately to account for existing facts of political behaviour and attitudes, and, at the same time, not endanger existing democratic systems by giving rise to unrealistic, and potentially disruptive, expectations. Eckstein, in his *A Theory of Stable Democracy* (1966), as the title implies, concentrates on the conditions, or prerequisites, necessary for a democratic system to maintain itself stably over time.

The definition of 'democracy' that Eckstein uses is the familiar one of a political system where elections decide the outcome of competition for policies and power[1] but if this system is to be stable then the form that

---

[1] Eckstein (1966, p. 229). Eckstein does not explicitly consider his theory in relation to 'classical' theory but one remark, at least, does indicate that he considers earlier theories to be inadequate. He says that, today, we need a more pessimistic approach to democratic government, not one based on the assumption that men are natural democrats, but one that focuses on the 'calamitously improbable' combination of necessary conditions (pp. 285–6).

government takes must be of a certain type. The 'stability' of the system refers not just to longevity—that could result by 'accident'—but survival because of a capacity for adjustment to change, realisation of political aspirations and the keeping of allegiances and it also implies that political decision-making is effective in the 'basic sense of action itself, any sort of action, in pursuit of shared goals or in adjustment to changing conditions' (p. 228).

Eckstein points out that the one aspect of social relations most obviously and immediately related to political behaviour has been neglected in the literature; that is

authority patterns in non-governmental social relationships, in families, schools, economic organisations and the like . . . it stands to reason that if any aspect of social life can directly affect government it is the experiences with authority that men have in other spheres of life, especially those that mould their personalities and those to which they normally devote most of their lives (p. 225).

The first proposition of his theory, one that applies to any method of government, is that 'a government will tend to be stable if its authority pattern is congruent with the other authority patterns of the society of which it is a part' (p. 234). Eckstein considers that in this context 'congruent' can have two senses, which we shall refer to as the strong and the weak. The stronger is the sense of 'identical' synonymous in Eckstein's term with 'close resemblance' (p. 234). This is not the sense applicable in a democracy because such a situation of congruency of authority structures would not be possible there, or at least, it would have 'the gravest dysfunctional consequences'. Certain authority structures simply cannot be democratised, for instance, those in which socialisation of the young occurs (family, school) for, although we might 'pretend' that these are democratic, too realistic a pretence would produce 'warped and ineffectual human beings'. Similarly, in economic organisations democracy might be 'imitated' or 'simulated' but even this, taken too far, would lead to 'consequences no one wants', and moreover, 'we certainly know that capitalist economic organisation and even certain kinds of public ownership . . . militate against a democratisation of economic relations'. Thus, it is just those spheres that Eckstein pointed out as most important for political behaviour that must, necessarily, be undemocratic (pp. 237–8). The weaker sense of 'congruence' is that of 'graduated resemblance'—a sense that makes 'stringent requirements but not requirements impossible to fulfill'. This sense is not entirely clear but Eckstein argues that some 'segments' of society are closer to government than others, either in the sense of being 'adult' or of being 'political'. There will be congruence in the weak sense if (a) authority patterns increase in similarity to government the 'closer' they are to it or, (b) there is a high degree of resemblance in patterns 'adjacent to government' and in distant segments functionally appropriate patterns have been departed from in favour of actual or ritual imitation of the government pattern.[1]

There might seem to be a difficulty in the theory here because stability can only be attained and 'strain' (a psychological state and social condition similar to that denoted by 'anomie') avoided if congruency is achieved. Strain can be minimised if there are sufficient opportunities for individuals to learn democratic patterns of action, particularly if the democratic authority structures are those closest to government or those that involve the political élites, i.e. if the weak sense of congruency is achieved. But Eckstein has already said that it is impossible to democratise some of the authority structures closest to government.[2] This, however, is not really a problem for the theory because Eckstein argues that, therefore, for stable democracy the governmental authority pattern must be made congruent with the prevailing form of authority structure in the society; that is, the governmental pattern must not be 'purely' democratic. It must contain a 'balance of disparate elements' and there must be a 'healthy element of authoritarianism'. He also advances two other reasons for the existence of the latter element: one is part of the definition of 'stability', effective decision-making can only take place if this element of authoritarianism is present; and the second is psychological, men have a need for firm (authoritarian) leaders and leadership, and this need must be satisfied if the stability of the system is to be maintained (pp. 262–7).

The conclusion of Eckstein's theory—which might be thought rather paradoxical given that the theory is a theory of democracy—is that for a *stable* democratic system the structure of authority in national government necessarily cannot be really, or at least 'purely', a democratic one.

A theory of democracy that is common to all four of these writers, and to many other theorists of democracy today, can now be briefly set out. I shall refer to this theory from now on as the contemporary theory of democracy. The theory, referred to as an empirical or descriptive one, focuses on the operation of the democratic political system as a whole and

---

[1] (pp. 238–40). (b) is the minimum condition for (meaning of) 'congruence'; (a) is, I take it, what Eckstein means by 'a graduated pattern in a proper segmentation of society' (p. 239).

[2] (pp. 254 ff.). Like Dahl, Eckstein says little about how the 'social training' takes place. Since most people are not very politically active and so will not be participating in the most 'congruent' authority structures (those 'closest' to government) they are being socialised into non-democratic patterns. Thus, Eckstein's theory supports the arguments of those who stress the dangers to the stability of the system of greater participation by the (non-democratic) majority.

is grounded in the facts of present-day political attitudes and behaviour as revealed by sociological investigation.

In the theory, 'democracy' refers to a political method or set of institutional arrangements at national level. The characteristically democratic element in the method is the competition of leaders (élites) for the votes of the people at periodic, free elections. Elections are crucial to the democratic method for it is primarily through elections that the majority can exercise control over their leaders. Responsiveness of leaders to non-élite demands, or 'control' over leaders, is ensured primarily through the sanction of loss of office at elections; the decisions of leaders can also be influenced by active groups bringing pressure to bear during inter-election periods. 'Political equality' in the theory refers to universal suffrage and to the existence of equality of opportunity of access to channels of influence over leaders. Finally, 'participation', so far as the majority is concerned, is participation in the choice of decision makers. Therefore, the function of participation in the theory is solely a protective one; the protection of the individual from arbitrary decisions by elected leaders and the protection of his private interests. It is in its achievement of this aim that the justification for the democratic method lies.

Certain conditions are necessary if the democratic system is to remain stable. The level of participation by the majority should not rise much above the minimum necessary to keep the democratic method (electoral machinery) working; that is, it should remain at about the level that exists at present in the Anglo-American democracies. The fact that non-democratic attitudes are relatively more common among the inactive means that any increase in participation by the apathetic would weaken the consensus on the norms of the democratic method, which is a further necessary condition. Although there is no definite 'democratic character' required of all citizens, the social training or socialisation in the democratic method that is necessary can take place inside existing, diverse, non-governmental authority structures. Providing that there is some degree of congruency between the structure of authority of government and non-governmental authority structures close to it, then stability can be maintained. As Bachrach (1967, p. 95) has noted, such a model of democracy can be seen as one where the majority (non-élites) gain maximum output (policy decisions) from leaders with the minimum input (participation) on their part.

The contemporary theory of democracy has gained almost universal support among present-day political theorists but it has not gone entirely uncriticised, although the critics' voices are rather muted.[1] The attack of

---

[1] Almost any recent piece of writing on democracy will furnish an example of the

the critics focuses on two major points. Firstly, they argue that the advocates of the contemporary theory of democracy have misunderstood the 'classical' theory; it was not primarily a descriptive theory as they imply, but a normative one, 'an essay in prescription' (Davis, 1964, p. 39). I shall examine this point shortly. Secondly, the critics argue that in the revision of the 'classical' theory the ideals contained in that theory have been rejected and replaced with others; 'the revisionists have fundamentally changed the normative significance of democracy' (Walker, 1966, p. 286).

It has already been emphasised that the contemporary theory is presented as a 'value-free', descriptive theory. Dahl (1966) has, indeed, explicitly rejected the charge that he, and other theorists, have produced a new normative theory. Here his critics have a better understanding of the nature of the contemporary theory than Dahl himself. Taylor (1967) points out that any political theory does its job by delineating from the phenomena under consideration those that need to be explained and those that are relevant to that explanation. But further, as Taylor has shown, this selection means not only that certain dimensions are ruled out as irrelevant —and these may be crucial for another theory—but also that the chosen dimensions support a normative position, a position implicit in the theory itself.

The contemporary theory of democracy does not merely describe the operation of certain political systems, but implies that this is the kind of system that we should value and includes a set of standards or criteria by which a political system may be judged 'democratic'. It is not difficult to see that, for the theorists under consideration, these standards are those that are inherent in the existing, Anglo-American democratic system and that with the development of this system we already have the ideal democratic polity. Berelson, for example, says that the existing (American) political system 'not only works on the most difficult and complex questions but often works with distinction' (1954, p. 312). Dahl concludes *A Preface to Democratic Theory* by remarking that although he had not attempted to determine whether the system he describes is a desirable one, nevertheless it does enable all active and legitimate groups to be heard at some stage in the decision-making process, 'which is no mean thing', and that it is also 'a relatively efficient system for reinforcing agreement, encouraging moderation, and maintaining social peace' (1956, pp. 149–51). Clearly,

contemporary theory, but see e.g. Almond and Verba (1965), Lipset (1960), Mayo (1960), Morris Jones (1954), Milbrath (1965), Plamenatz (1958). For examples of criticisms of the contemporary theory see Bachrach (1967), Bay (1965), Davis (1964), Duncan and Lukes (1963), Goldschmidt (1966), Rousseas and Farganis (1963), Walker (1966).

a political system that can and does tackle difficult questions with distinction, that can and does ensure social peace, *is* inherently desirable. Furthermore, by ruling out certain dimensions, the contemporary theory presents us with two alternatives; a system where leaders are controlled by, and accountable to the electorate, and where the latter have a choice between competing leaders or élites—and a system where this is not the case ('totalitarianism'). But the choice is made by the presentation of the alternatives; we do have a choice between competing leaders, therefore the system that we ought to have is the very one that we do in fact have.

The critics, then, are right in their contention that the contemporary theory not only has its own normative content but that it implies that we—or, at least, Anglo-Saxon Westerners—are living in the 'ideal' democratic system. They are also right to say that in so far as the ideal contained in the 'classical' theory differed from existing realities then this ideal has been rejected. The critics of the contemporary theory agree broadly on what this other ideal was. All agree that maximum participation by all the people was central to it; more generally, as Davis (1964) puts it, it was the ideal of 'rational and active and informed democratic man' (p. 29). But though they agree on the content of the ideal only one of the critics, Bachrach, even begins to address himself to the crucial question of whether the theorists of contemporary democracy are not right, given the available empirical facts, to reject this ideal. As Duncan and Lukes (1963, p. 160) point out, empirical evidence can lead us to change normative theories under certain circumstances, although they add that as far as changing the ideal is concerned 'it needs to be shown exactly how and why the ideal is rendered improbable or impossible of attainment. This has nowhere been done'. But neither, on the other hand, have the critics of the contemporary theory shown how or why the ideal *is* attainable.[1] Perhaps Sartori is right to argue that it is a mistake to look for reasons for the lack of interest and activity in politics on the part of the majority; perhaps the theorists of contemporary democracy are right to stress the fragility of democratic political systems and the 'calamitous improbability' that the right combination of prerequisites for stability will occur in more than a few countries, if at all.

The reason for the inconclusive nature of the criticisms of the contemporary theory of democracy lies in the fact that the critics, too, have accepted Schumpeter's formulation of the problem. They tend to accept the characterisation of the 'classical' theory by the writers whom they

---

[1] Bachrach (1967) indicates why we should retain the ideal but gives only the most very general suggestions as to how to set about realising it, and no evidence to show whether this is possible.

are criticising, and like them, tend to present a composite model of that theory without giving the sources from which it is derived or refer undiscriminatingly to a very diverse list of theorists.[1] More importantly, they do not question the existence of this theory even though they disagree about its nature. What neither its critics or its defenders have realised is that *the notion of a 'classical theory of democracy' is a myth*. Neither side in the controversy has done the obvious, and the necessary, and looked in detail at what the earlier theorists did in fact have to say. Because of this the myth of a 'classical' theory continues and the views and the nature of the theories of the earlier writers on democracy are persistently misrepresented. Only when the myth has been exposed can the question be tackled of whether the normative revision of democracy is justified or not. It is to the myth that we now turn.

The first thing that has to be done is to come to some decision about who these elusive classical theorists are. Clearly, there is a wide range of names from which one could choose, and to make the choice we shall start in the obvious place; with Schumpeter's definition of classical democracy. He defined the classical democratic method as 'that institutional arrangement for arriving at political decisions which realises the common good by making the people itself decide issues through the election of individuals who are to assemble in order to carry out its will' (1943, p. 250). Schumpeter refers to the 'classical' theory as an 'eighteenth century' theory and says that it developed from a small-scale prototype; he also calls it 'utilitarian' (pp. 248 and 267). So, taking these remarks as a guide, we arrive at the names of Rousseau, the two Mills and Bentham, all of whom have a good claim to the title of 'classical' theorist of democracy. But if the identification of the theory of any one of these writers with Schumpeter's definition looks dubious, to imply that the theories of all of them, and perhaps of other writers as well, can somehow be mixed to reveal it, is an even more curious suggestion. Schumpeter argues that for this political method to work 'everyone would have to know definitely what he wants to stand for . . . a clear *and prompt* conclusion as to particular issues would have to be derived according to the rules of logical inference . . . all this the model citizen would have to perform for himself and independently of pressure groups and propaganda' (p. 253–4). He makes two main

---

[1] Duncan and Lukes are an exception, they do take J. S. Mill as their example of a 'classical' theorist. Walker, after objecting that it is usually unclear which theorists are being referred to, then goes on to present a brief account of the 'classical' theory drawn largely from Davis's article in which the latter, though giving a very diverse list of writers, does not indicate in the text from which specific theorists he draws his material. Bachrach also refers indiscriminately to 'classical theorists'.

criticisms of the 'classical' theory that are of particular relevance here. Firstly that it is quite unrealistic and demands a level of rationality from the ordinary man that is just not possible. To the ordinary man, he says, anticipating Sartori, only things of which he has everyday experience are fully 'real', and politics does not usually fall into this category. On the whole when the ordinary man has to deal with political affairs 'the sense of reality is . . . completely lost' and he drops to a 'lower level of mental performance as soon as he enters the political field'. Secondly he argues that the 'classical' theory virtually ignored leadership (pp. 258–61 and 270). If Schumpeter's characterisation of the 'classical' theory, and what it requires from the ordinary citizen were correct, then, no doubt, there would be a good deal of validity in his criticisms. But Schumpeter not only misrepresents what the so-called classical theorists had to say but he has not realised that two very different theories about democracy are to be found in their writings. To support this contention the work of the four 'classical' theorists has to be examined. At this point only Bentham and James Mill will be, briefly, considered. The theories of Rousseau and J. S. Mill will be dealt with in detail in the next chapter.

Bentham and James Mill provide examples of writers from whose theories one could extract something which bears a family resemblance to Schumpeter's definition of the 'classical' theory. Bentham, in his later writings, where he advocated universal suffrage, the secret ballot and annual parliaments, expected the electorate to exercise a fair degree of control over their representatives. He wished the latter to be called 'deputies'; by that word, he said, 'a plain matter of fact is indicated and *that* the appropriate one'[1] and the 'locative' and 'dislocative' functions were the most important that the electorate performed. This does imply that, on most issues, the electorate have an opinion as to which policies are in their, and the universal, interest, and hence an opinion on which policies their delegate should vote for. For Bentham and Mill the 'people' meant the 'numerous classes', the only body capable of acting as a check against the pursuit of 'sinister' interests by the government. Bentham argued that because the citizen's interest is in security against bad government so he will act accordingly and 'for the gratification of any sinister desire at the expense of the universal interest he cannot hope to find co-operation and support from any considerable number of his fellow citizens'.[2] James Mill said that the people's sympathies are with one another, 'not with those exterior parties whose interests come into competition with theirs'.[3]

[1] Bentham (1843), vol. IX, bk. II, ch. v, §I p. 155.
[2] Bentham (1843), vol. IX, bk. I, ch. xv, §IV, p. 100.
[3] Quoted in Hamburger (1965, p. 54).

Now, in view of this one could perhaps draw the inference that the two theorists expected that electors would make each decision independently of 'propaganda' and form their opinions 'logically', as Schumpeter says, but neither writer expected that opinions would be formed in a vacuum. Indeed, Bentham laid great stress on public opinion and the need for the individual to take account of it and he pointed out one advantage of an elector in a democracy, that 'into no company can he enter without seeing those who . . . are ready to communicate to him whatever they know, have seen, or heard, or think. The annals of the year . . . the pictures of all public functionaries . . . find a place on his table in company with his daily bread'.[1] Mill stressed the importance of educating the electorate into socially responsible voting and he thought that the main aspect of this education lay in the fact that the working classes did take the 'wise and virtuous' middle classes as their reference group when forming their opinions and so would vote responsibly. Neither Mill nor Bentham shared quite the view of the electorate imputed to them by Schumpeter.[2] More importantly, their main concern was with the choice of good representatives (leaders) rather than the formulation of the electorate's opinions as such. Bentham expected that those citizens least qualified to judge a prospective representative's moral and intellectual qualities would ask the advice of the competent and that the representative himself would, on occasion, influence his constituents by his speeches; he is there to further the universal interest. It would be possible for the electorate to choose the best representative without their holding the sort of 'logical' principles that Schumpeter suggested. The fact that Bentham and Mill expected each citizen to be interested in politics because it was in his best interest to be so (and thought that he could be educated to see this) is not incompatible with some kind of 'influence' being brought to bear, nor does it imply that each citizen makes a discrete decision on each item of policy, logically based on all the evidence, in complete isolation from all his other decisions and from the opinions of others.

Nevertheless, there is, as noted, a similarity between the theories of James Mill and Bentham and Schumpeter's 'classical' theory, and for a very significant reason. Like the latter, Mill and Bentham are concerned almost entirely with the national 'institutional arrangements' of the political system. The participation of the people has a very narrow function; it ensures that good government, i.e. 'government in the universal

---

[1] Bentham (1843), vol. IX, bk. I, ch. XV, §v, p. 102. For the importance of public opinion in Bentham's theory see Wolin (1961, p. 346).

[2] Wolin (1961, p. 332) emphasises the role of the passions as well as that of reason in the utilitarian theories.

interest', is achieved through the sanction of loss of office. For Bentham and Mill participation thus had a purely protective function, it ensured that the private interests of each citizen were protected (the universal interest being merely a sum of individual interests). Their theories can be classified as 'democratic' because they thought that the 'numerous classes' only were capable of defending the universal interest and thus advocated the participation (voting and discussion) of all the people.[1] However, other theorists have held that participation is necessary because of its protective function without regarding it as necessary that *all* the people should, therefore, participate. There is nothing specifically democratic about this view of the function of participation. It plays, for example, a similar role in Locke's theory—who was far from being a democrat (even though he has been claimed as one of the ubiquitious 'classical democrats' by Milbrath).[2]

As we have seen, the formulators of the contemporary theory of democracy also regard participation exclusively as a protective device. In their view the 'democratic' nature of the system rests primarily on the form of the national 'institutional arrangements', specifically on the competition of leaders (potential representatives) for votes, so that theorists who hold this view of the role of participation are, first and foremost, theorists of representative government. This is, of course, an important aspect of democratic theory; it would be absurd to try to deny this, or to question the influential contribution of Bentham—or Locke—to the theory and practice of democracy today. The point is, however, that the theory of representative government is not the whole of democratic theory as much recent work would suggest. The very importance of Schumpeter's influence is that it has obscured the fact that not all writers who have claim to be called 'classical' theorists of democracy took the same view of the role of participation. In the theories of J. S. Mill and Rousseau, for example, participation has far wider functions and is central to the establishment and maintenance of a democratic polity, the latter being regarded not just as a set of national representative institutions but what I shall call a participatory society (the significance of that phrase will be made clear in the next chapter). I shall, therefore, refer to theorists like Rousseau as theorists of participatory democracy.

Because this difference exists it is nonsense to speak of one 'classical'

[1] Hamburger (1962) argues convincingly that Mill was not in favour of restricting the suffrage to the middle classes as is often claimed.
[2] Milbrath (1965, p. 143). From the description he gives of Locke's theory he appears to have confused him with Rousseau! For this aspect of Locke's political theory see, e.g. Seliger (1968), chs. 10 and 11. Hegel, too gives participation a philosophical justification in his political theory, and Burke allows that it is necessary for good government, but neither of these writers includes all the people in the electorate.

theory of democracy. It is because they, too, subscribe to the classical myth that the critics of the contemporary theory of democracy have never explained exactly what the role of participation in the earlier theories is or why such a high value was placed upon it in—some—theories. This can only be done by a detailed examination of the theories concerned. Davis (1964) has said that the 'classical' theory (i.e. the theory of participatory democracy) had an ambitious purpose, 'the education of an entire people to the point where their intellectual, emotional, and moral capacities have reached their full potential and they are joined, freely and actively in a genuine community', and that the strategy for reaching this end is through the use of 'political activity and government for the purpose of public education'. However, he goes on to say that the 'unfinished business' of democratic theory is 'the elaboration of plans of action and specific prescriptions which offer hope of progress towards a genuinely democratic polity' (pp. 40 and 41). It is exactly this last that can be found in the theories of the writers on participatory democracy; a set of specific prescriptions and plans of action necessary for the attainment of political democracy. This does take place through 'public education' but the latter depends on participation in many spheres of society on 'political activity' in a very wide sense of that term.[1]

Until the theory of participatory democracy has been examined in detail and the possibilities for its empirical realisation assessed, we do not know how much 'unfinished business', or of what sort, remains for democratic theory. The first step in this task is to consider the work of three theorists of participatory democracy. The first are Rousseau and John Stuart Mill, two examples of 'classical' democratic theorists, whose theories provide us with the basic postulates of a theory of participatory democracy. The third is G. D. H. Cole, a twentieth-century political theorist, in whose early writings can be found a detailed plan for a participatory society in the form of Guild Socialism. However, this plan is, in itself, of minor importance; Cole's work is of significance because he developed a theory of participatory democracy that not only included and extended those basic postulates, but was set in the context of a modern, large-scale, industrialised society.

---

[1] Bachrach (1967), ch. 7, argues for a wide interpretation of 'political' but has not realised that this is linked to the arguments of the earlier theorists. Thus, he incorrectly remarks that 'in underscoring the importance of widespread participation in political decision making, ['classical' theory] offers no realistic guidelines as to how its prescription is to be filled in large urban societies' (p. 99).

CHAPTER II

Rousseau, John Stuart Mill and
G. D. H. Cole: a participatory theory of democracy

Rousseau might be called the theorist *par excellence* of participation, and an understanding of the nature of the political system that he describes in *The Social Contract* is vital for the theory of participatory democracy. Rousseau's entire political theory hinges on the individual participation of each citizen in political decision making and in his theory participation is very much more than a protective adjunct to a set of institutional arrangements; it also has a psychological effect on the participants, ensuring that there is a continuing interrelationship between the working of institutions and the psychological qualities and attitudes of individuals interacting within them. It is their stress on this aspect of participation and its place at the centre of their theories that marks the distinctive contribution of the theorists of participatory democracy to democratic theory as a whole. Although Rousseau was writing before the modern institutions of democracy were developed, and his ideal society is a non-industrial city-state, it is in his theory that the basic hypotheses about the function of participation in a democratic polity can be found.[1]

In order to understand the role of participation in Rousseau's political theory it is essential to be clear about the nature of his ideal, participatory political system, as this has been subject to widely differing interpretations. Firstly, Rousseau argued that certain economic conditions were necessary for a participatory system. As is well known Rousseau advocated a society made up of small, peasant proprietors, i.e. he advocated a society of economic equality and economic independence. His theory does not require absolute equality as is often implied, but rather that the differences that do exist should not lead to political inequality. Ideally, there should

---

[1] The political system described in *The Social Contract* was not a democracy according to Rousseau's usage of the term. For him, a 'democracy' was a system where the citizens executed as well as made the laws and for that reason it was fit only for gods (bk. III, ch. 4). It might be noted here that as Rousseau's is a direct, not representative system, it does *not* conform to Schumpeter's definition of 'classical' democratic theory.

be a situation where 'no citizen shall be rich enough to buy another and none so poor as to be forced to sell himself' and the vital requirement is for each man to own some property—the most sacred of the citizen's rights—because the security and independence that this gives to the individual is the necessary basis on which rest his political equality and political independence.[1]

If these conditions are established the citizens can assemble as equal and independent individuals, yet Rousseau also wanted them to be inter-dependent, the latter being necessary if the independence and equality are to be preserved. This is not so paradoxical as it sounds because the partici-patory situation is such that each citizen would be powerless to do any-thing without the co-operation of all the others, or of the majority. Each citizen would be, as he puts it, 'excessively dependent on the republic' (1968, p. 99, bk. II, ch. 12), i.e. there would be an equal dependence of each individual on all the others viewed collectively as sovereign, and independent participation is the mechanism whereby this interdependence is enforced. The way in which it works is both simple and subtle. It is possible to read the *Social Contract* as an elaboration of the idea that laws, not men, should rule, but an even better formulation of the role of participation is that men are to be ruled by the logic of the operation of the political situation that they had themselves created and that this situation was such that the possibility of the rule of individual men was 'automatically' precluded. It is because the citizens are independent equals, not dependent on anyone else for their vote or opinion, that in the political assembly no one need vote for any policy that is not as much to his advantage as to the advantage of any other. Individual X will be unable to persuade others to vote for his proposal that gives X alone some advantage. In a crucial passage in the *Social Contract* Rousseau asks 'how should it be that the general will is always rightful and that all men con-stantly wish the happiness of each but for the fact that there is no one who does not take that word "each" to pertain to himself and in voting for all think of himself?'[2] In other words, the only policy that will be acceptable to all is the one where any benefits and burdens are equally shared; the participatory process ensures that political equality is made effective in the decision-making assembly. The substantive policy result is that the general will is, tautologically, always just (i.e. affects all equally) so that at the same time individual rights and interests are protected and the public

[1] Rousseau (1968), bk. II, ch. 11, p. 96, and (1913), p. 254.
[2] Rousseau (1968), bk. II, ch. 4, p. 75. See also p. 76, 'the general will is an institution in which each necessarily submits himself to the same conditions which he imposes on others.'

interest furthered. The law has 'emerged' from the participatory process and it is the law, not men, that governs individual actions.[1]

Rousseau thought that the ideal situation for decision making was one where no organised groups were present, just individuals, because the former might be able to make their 'particular wills' prevail. Rousseau's remarks about groups follow directly from what he says about the operation of the participatory process. He recognised that there would inevitably be 'tacit associations', i.e. unorganised individuals who were united by some common interest, but it would be very difficult for such a tacit association to obtain support for a policy to its special advantage because of the conditions under which participation takes place (1913, p. 237). If it was impossible to avoid organised associations within the community then, Rousseau argues, these should be as numerous and as equal in political power as possible. That is, the participatory situation of individuals would be repeated so far as the groups were concerned, and none could gain at the expense of the rest. Rousseau says nothing, not surprisingly, about the internal authority structure of such groups but his basic analysis of the participatory process can be applied to any group or association.[2]

This analysis of the operation of Rousseau's participatory system makes two points clear; first, that 'participation' for Rousseau is participation in the making of decisions and second, that it is, as in theories of representative government, a way of protecting private interests and ensuring good government. But participation is also considerably more than this in Rousseau's theory. Plamenatz (1963) has said of Rousseau that 'he turns our minds . . . to considering how the social order affects the structure of human personality' (vol. i, p. 440), and it is the psychological impact of social and political institutions that is Rousseau's main concern; which aspect of men's characters do particular institutions develop? The crucial variable here is whether or not the institution is a participatory one and the central function of participation in Rousseau's theory is an educative one, using the term 'education' in the widest sense. Rousseau's ideal system is designed to develop responsible, individual social and political action

---

[1] Apropos of Schumpeter's 'classical' definition it is something of a misnomer to say that Rousseau's citizens decide 'issues'. What they do by participating is to come up with the right answer to a problem (i.e. the general will). There will not necessarily be a right answer in the case of an 'issue' as we understand the term in the political conditions of today. Nor is an ability to make 'logical inferences' required. Quite the contrary, the whole point of the participatory situation is that each independent but interdependent individual is 'forced' to appreciate that there is only one right answer, to apply the word 'each' to himself.

[2] Rousseau (1968), bk. ii, ch. 3, p. 73. See also Barry (1964).

through the effect of the participatory process. During this process the individual learns that the word 'each' must be applied to himself; that is to say, he finds that he has to take into account wider matters than his own immediate private interests if he is to gain co-operation from others, and he learns that the public and private interest are linked. The logic of the operation of the participatory system is such that he is 'forced' to deliberate according to his sense of justice, according to what Rousseau calls his 'constant will' because fellow citizens can always resist the implementation of inequitable demands. As a result of participating in decision making the individual is educated to distinguish between his own impulses and desires, he learns to be a public as well as a private citizen.[1] Rousseau also believes that through this educative process the individual will eventually come to feel little or no conflict between the demands of the public and private spheres. Once the participatory system is established, and this is a point of major importance, it becomes self-sustaining because the very qualities that are required of individual citizens if the system is to work successfully are those that the process of participation itself develops and fosters; the more the individual citizen participates the better able he is to do so. The human results that accrue through the participatory process provide an important justification for a participatory system.

Another aspect of the role of participation in Rousseau's theory is the close connection between participation and control and this is bound up with his notion of freedom. A full discussion of Rousseau's use of this latter concept is not necessary here, but it is inextricably bound up with the process of participation. Perhaps the most famous, or notorious, words that Rousseau ever wrote were that a man might be 'forced to be free' and he also defined freedom as 'obedience to a law one prescribes to oneself'.[2] Some of the more fanciful and sinister interpretations that have been placed on the first words would not have been possible if Rousseau's concept of freedom had been placed firmly in the context of participation, for the way in which an individual can be 'forced' to be free is part and

[1] The setting up of situations that 'force' the individual to learn for himself is the basis of the whole of Rousseau's theory of education, c.f. the remarks on *Émile* and the *Nouvelle Héloïse* in Shklar (1964). The additional methods of educating the citizenry advocated by Rousseau (e.g. public ceremonies) would seem to derive from his pessimism; they are not a necessary part of the theory. At most they work in the same direction as participation and do not substitute for it. The institution of the law-giver can be seen as an answer to the problem of how the initial step into a participatory situation is to be taken, but on Rousseau's own arguments the self-sustaining nature of the participatory political system should make it an exception to his view that all governments tend in the end to 'degenerate'.
[2] Rousseau (1968), bk. I, ch. 7, p. 64, and bk. I, ch. 8, p. 65.

parcel of the same process by which he is 'forcibly' educated through participating in decision making. Rousseau argues that unless each individual is 'forced' through the participatory process into socially responsible action then there can be no law which ensures everyone's freedom, i.e. there can be no general will or the kind of just law that the individual can prescribe to himself. While the subjective element in Rousseau's concept of freedom—that under such a law the individual will feel unconstrained, will *feel* free—has often been commented upon, it is usually overlooked that there is an objective element involved as well. (Though this is not to say that one accepts Rousseau's definition of freedom as consisting in obedience.) The individual's actual, as well as his sense of, freedom is increased through participation in decision making because it gives him a very real degree of *control* over the course of his life and the structure of his environment. Rousseau also argues that freedom requires that he should exercise a fair measure of control over those that execute the laws and over representatives if an indirect system is necessary.[1] In the introduction to his recent translation of the *Social Contract* Cranston criticises Rousseau for never, in that work, seeing institutions as a threat to freedom (Rousseau, 1968, p. 41). This criticism precisely misses the point. The participatory institutions of the *Social Contract* cannot be a threat to freedom just because of the logic of their operation, because of the interrelationship between the authority structure of institutions and the psychological orientations of individuals. It is the whole point of Rousseau's argument that the (existing) non-participatory institutions do pose such a threat, indeed, they make freedom impossible—men are everywhere 'in chains'. The ideal institutions described in the *Social Contract* are ideal because Rousseau regards their operation as guaranteeing freedom.

Rousseau also sees participation as increasing the value of his freedom to the individual by enabling him to be (and remain) his own master. Like the rest of Rousseau's theory the notion of 'being one's own master' has come in for a good deal of criticism, although Cranston strikes a new note when he refers to it as the ideal of a footman and so, presumably, not worth serious consideration—but that is too easy a dismissal of the idea.[2]

---

[1] See Rousseau (1968, bk. III, ch. 18, p. 148) and (1953, pp. 192 ff.).

[2] Rousseau (1968, p. 42). The more familiar criticism of the idea is that it is potentially 'totalitarian' or at least unlibertarian, and that it has little to do with the notion of 'negative' freedom which, in turn, is often held to be the only form of freedom compatible with democracy. It is clear that this discussion implicitly rejects the idea that there are two different concepts of freedom and that Rousseau is an unequivocal advocate of the 'positive' notion. It also rejects the view that in talking of being one's own master Rousseau is referring only to mastery of one's 'lower nature'. This element is present in Rousseau but to suggest that it is the whole of his theory is

In the eighth *Letter from the Mountain* Rousseau says that freedom consists 'moins à faire sa volonté qu'a n'être pas soumis à celle d'autrui; elle consiste encore à ne pas soumetre la volonté d'autrui à la nôtre. Quiconque est maître ne peut être libre'. (1965, vol. II, p. 234). That is, one must not be master of another; when one is master of oneself and one's life, however, then freedom is enhanced through the control over that life that is required before it is possible to describe the individual as his 'own master'. Secondly, the participatory process ensures that although no man, or group, is master of another, all are equally dependent on each other and equally subject to the law. The (impersonal) rule of law that is made possible through participation and its connection with 'being one's own master' gives us further insight into the reason why Rousseau thinks that individuals will conscientiously accept a law arrived at through a participatory decision-making process. More generally, it is now possible to see that a second function of participation in Rousseau's theory is that it enables collective decisions to be more easily accepted by the individual.

Rousseau also suggests that participation has a third, integrative function; that it increases the feeling among individual citizens that they 'belong' in their community. In a sense integration derives from all the factors mentioned already. For example, the basic economic equality means that there is no disruptive division between rich and poor, there are no men like the one Rousseau disapprovingly mentions in *Émile* who, when asked which was his country, replied 'I am one of the rich' (1911, p. 313). More important is the experience of participation in decision making itself, and the complex totality of results to which it is seen to lead, both for the individual and for the whole political system; this experience attaches the individual to his society and is instrumental in developing it into a true community.

This examination of Rousseau's political theory has provided us with the argument that there is an interrelationship between the authority structures of institutions and the psychological qualities and attitudes of individuals, and with the related argument that the major function of participation is an educative one. These arguments form the basis of the theory of participatory democracy as will become clear from the discussion of the theories of J. S. Mill and Cole. The theories of these two writers reinforce Rousseau's arguments about participation but more interestingly in these theories the theory of participatory democracy is lifted out of the context of a city-state of peasant proprietors into that of a modern political system.

extremely misleading. Such an interpretation is only possible if the whole participatory context of Rousseau's discussion of freedom is ignored. For the interpretation criticised see especially Berlin (1958); also Talmon (1952).

John Stuart Mill, in his social and political theory, as in other matters, started out as a devoted adherent of the doctrines of his father and of Bentham, which he later severely criticised, so that he provides an excellent example of the differences between the theories of representative government and participatory democracy. However, Mill never completely rejected these early teachings and by the end of his life his political theory was composed of a mixture of all the diverse influences that had affected him. He never managed satisfactorily to synthesise these—the task is probably an impossible one—and this means that there is a profound ambiguity between the participatory foundations of his theory and some of his more practical proposals for the establishment of his 'ideally best polity'.

Echoes of the utilitarian view of the purely protective function of participation can be found in Mill's mature political theory. For example, he says in *Representative Government*—which expressed the principles 'to which I have been working up during the greater part of my life'—that one of the greatest dangers of democracy lies in 'the sinister interest of the holders of power: it is the danger of class legislation . . . And one of the most important questions demanding consideration . . . is how to provide efficacious securities against this evil'.[1] For Mill, however, Bentham's notion of 'good government' only dealt with part of the problem. Mill distinguished two aspects of good government. First, 'how far it promotes the good management of the affairs of society by means of the existing faculties, moral, intellectual, and active, of its various members' and this criterion of good government relates to government seen as 'a set of organised arrangements for public business' (1910, pp. 208 and 195). Mill criticised Bentham for building his political theory on the assumption that this aspect was the whole. He wrote in the essay on *Bentham* that all that the latter could do

is but to indicate means by which in any given state of the national mind, the material interests of society can be protected; . . . (his theory) can teach the means of organising and regulating the merely *business* part of the social arrangements . . . He committed the mistake of supposing that the *business* part of human affairs was the whole of them (Mill's emphasis) (1963, p. 102).

In J. S. Mill's estimation the merely business aspect of government is the least important; fundamental is government in its second aspect, that of 'a great influence acting on the human mind', and the criterion to be used to judge political institutions in this light is 'the degree in which they promote the general mental advancement of the community, including

[1] Mill (1910) Preface and p. 254. For an account of the 'working up' see Burns (1957).

under that phrase advancement in intellect, in virtue, and in practical activity and efficiency' (1910, p. 195). In this respect Bentham's theory has nothing to say. Mill sees government and political institutions first and foremost as educative in the broadest sense of that word. For him the two aspects of government are interrelated in that a necessary condition of good government in the first, business, sense is the promotion of the right kind of individual character and for this the right kind of institutions are necessary (1963, p. 102). It is primarily for this reason, not because such a form of government will be in the universal interest, that Mill regards popular, democratic government as the 'ideally best polity'. Thus, he is against a benevolent despotism, which as he points out, could, if it were all-seeing, ensure that the 'business' side of government were properly carried out, because, as he asks, 'what sort of human beings can be formed under such a regimen? What development can either their thinking or their active faculties attain under it? . . . Their moral capacities are equally stunted. Wherever the sphere of action of human beings is artificially circumscribed, their sentiments are narrowed and dwarfed . . .' (1910, pp. 203–4).

It is only within a context of popular, participatory institutions that Mill sees an 'active', public-spirited type of character being fostered. Here, again, we find the basic assertion of the theorists of participatory democracy of the interrelationship and connection between individuals, their qualities and psychological characteristics, and types of institutions; the assertion that responsible social and political action depends largely on the sort of institutions within which the individual has, politically, to act. Like Rousseau, Mill sees these qualities being as much developed by participation as existing beforehand and thus the political system has a self-sustaining character.[1] Nor does Mill regard it as necessary that citizens should perform the sort of logical and rational calculations that Schumpeter asserted were necessary. He remarks in *Representative Government* that it would not be a rational form of government that required 'exalted' principles of conduct to motivate men, though he assumes that there is a certain level of political sophistication and public-spiritedness in the 'advanced' countries to whom this theory is addressed (1910, p. 253). Mill sees the educative function of participation in much the same terms

---

[1] Duncan and Lukes (1963, p. 160) note the self-sustaining character of the system but say that this arises through the possession of legal rights which leads men to become capable of exercising them, and thus to approach 'moral autonomy'. It is, of course, Mill's argument that it is the exercise not the possession that is important. Without participatory institutions the mere possession of legal rights would have little effect on character.

as Rousseau. He argues that where the individual is concerned solely with his own private affairs and does not participate in public affairs then the 'self-regarding' virtues suffer, as well as the capacities for responsible public action remaining undeveloped. 'The man never thinks of any collective interest, of any object to be pursued jointly with others, but only in competition with them, and in some measure at their expense' (1910, p. 217). The 'private money-getting occupation' of most individuals uses few of their faculties and tends to 'fasten his attention and interest exclusively upon himself, and upon his family as an appendage of himself; —making him indifferent to the public . . . and in his inordinate regard for his personal comforts, selfish and cowardly' (1963, p. 230). The whole situation is changed, however, when the individual can participate in public affairs; Mill, like Rousseau, saw the individual in this case being 'forced' to widen his horizons and to take the public interest into account. That is, the individual has to 'weigh interests not his own; to be guided, in the case of conflicting claims, by another rule than his private partialities; to apply, at every turn, principles and maxims which have for their reason of existence the common good' (1910, p. 217).

So far, Mill's theory has been shown to reinforce rather than add to Rousseau's hypothesis about the educative function of participation but there is another facet of Mill's theory which does add a further dimension to that hypothesis, a necessary dimension if the theory is to be applied to a large-scale society. I have already quoted from one of Mill's reviews of de Tocqueville's *Democracy in America*. This work was a decisive influence on Mill's political theory, in particular with the part which deals with local political institutions.[1] Mill was very impressed with de Tocqueville's discussion of centralisation and the dangers inherent in the development of a mass society (dangers made familiar now by modern sociologists also impressed by that analysis). In the *Political Economy* Mill declares that 'a democratic constitution not supported by democratic institutions in detail, but confined to the central government, not only is not political freedom, but often creates a spirit precisely the reverse'.[2] In his review of Volume II of de Tocqueville's book Mill argues that it is no use having universal suffrage and participation in national government if the individual has not been prepared for this participation at local level; it is at this level that he learns how to govern himself. 'A political act, to be done only once in a few years, and for which nothing in the daily habits of the citizen has prepared him, leaves his intellect and his moral dispositions very much as it found them' (1963, p. 229). In other words, if

[1] See Mill (1924, pp. 162–4) and Robson (1968, p. 106).
[2] Mill (1965), bk. v, ch. XI, §6, p. 944.

individuals in a large state are to be able to participate effectively in the government of the 'great society' then the necessary qualities underlying this participation have to be fostered and developed at the local level. Thus, for Mill, it is at local level where the real educative effect of participation occurs, where not only do the issues dealt with directly affect the individual and his everyday life but where he also stands a good chance of, himself, being elected to serve on a local body (1910, p. 347–8). It is by participating at the local level that the individual 'learns democracy'. 'We do not learn to read or write, to ride or swim, by being merely told how to do it, but by doing it, so it is only by practising popular government on a limited scale, that the people will ever learn how to exercise it on a larger' (1963, p. 186).

In a large-scale society representative government will be necessary and it is here that a difficulty arises; are Mill's practical proposals about representation compatible with the fundamental role he assigns to the educative function of participation in his theory? In his practical proposals Mill does not take his own arguments about participation seriously enough and this is largely because of ideas about the 'natural' state of society which are mixed in with the rest of his social and political theory.

Bentham and James Mill had thought that education, in the narrow, 'academic' sense of that term, was the major way of ensuring responsible political participation on the part of the 'numerous classes', and John Stuart Mill never really rejected this view. One of Mill's main concerns was how a political system could be achieved where the power was in the hands of an élite—the educated élite (in the narrow sense). A well cultivated intellect, he thought, was usually accompanied by 'prudence, temperance, and justice, and generally by all the virtues which are important in our intercourse with others'.[1] It was persons already well educated (the 'instructed') that Mill regarded as the 'wisest and best' men and whom he thought should be elected to office at all political levels. He considered that democracy was inevitable in the modern world, the problem was to so organise things that democratic political institutions would be compatible with the 'natural' state of society, a state where 'worldly power and moral influence are habitually exercised by the fittest persons whom the existing state of society affords' and where the 'multitude' have faith in this 'instructed' minority who will rule.[2] Mill, it should be noted, did not want a situation where the multitude was deferential in the unthinking,

[1] Quoted in Robson (1967, p. 210).
[2] Mill (1963, p. 17). Mill contrasts this state to the present one, a state of 'transition' where old institutions and doctrines have been 'outgrown' and the multitude have lost their faith in the instructed and are 'without a guide' (p. 3).

habitual sense of that word. Indeed, he thought that the time was past when such a thing was possible; 'the poor have come out of their leading strings ... whatever advice, exhortation, or guidance is held out to the labouring classes, must henceforth be tendered to them as equals and accepted by them with their eyes open'.[1] The élite had to be accountable to the many and it was the reconciliation of élite rule with accountability that Mill saw as the 'grand difficulty' in politics.[2] His answer to this problem gives rise to the ambiguity in his theory of participation.

From Mill's theory about the educative function of participation one would expect his answer to this problem would be that the maximum amount of opportunity should be given to the labouring classes to participate at local level so they would develop the necessary qualities and skills to enable them to assess the activities of representatives and hold them accountable. But Mill says nothing of the sort. His practical proposals for achieving a 'natural' but ideal political system are quite different. Mill distinguished between 'true democracy', which gives representation to minorities (and to this end Mill enthusiastically espoused Hare's proportional representation scheme), and the ideal system. The former did not solve the problem of ensuring that his educated élite had a preponderant influence; that ideal system could only come about under a system of plural voting based on educational attainment, 'though everyone ought to have a voice—that everyone should have an equal voice is a totally different proposition'.[3] Thus, Mill rejects Rousseau's argument that for effective participation political equality is necessary. Mill also implicitly uses a different definition of 'participation' from Rousseau, for he did not think that even the elected representatives should legislate but only accept or reject legislation prepared by a special commission appointed by the Crown; the proper job of representatives is discussion (1910, p. 235 ff.).

A further illustration of this point is Mill's comment on the form that the ideal suffrage should take. He says that it is 'by political discussion that the manual labourer, whose employment is a routine, and whose way of life brings him in contact with no variety of impressions, circumstances, or ideas, is taught that remote causes, and events which take place far off, have a most sensible effect even on his personal interests' (1910, p. 278).

One might raise the question, with Mill's practical proposals for the

[1] Mill (1965), bk. IV, ch. VII, §2, p. 763.
[2] See Hamburger (1965, p. 86). Mill's emphasis on the instructed minority illustrates how misconceived is Schumpeter's charge that the 'classical' theorists ignored leadership.
[3] Mill (1910, p. 283). In his *Autobiography* Mill admitted that the proposal for plural voting found favour with nobody (1924, p. 218).

achievement of the ideally best polity and his implicit definition of participation, of whether participation would have the educative effect he
postulated. The important point about Rousseau's paradigm of direct
participation is that the participatory process was organised in such a way
that individuals were, so to speak, psychologically 'open' to its effects.
But none of this obtains in Mill. The majority are branded by the suffrage
system as political inferiors and cannot resist the implementation of dis-
advantageous policies; if a predetermined élite are to gain political power
why should the majority even be interested in discussion? Mill seems unaware of any inconsistency in the various elements of his theory but it is
difficult to see how his kind of participation is to fulfil its allotted role. Even
with universal suffrage and decision making by representatives there would
not be such a 'strongly' educative environment as that provided by Rousseau's direct participatory system and the problem of how far Rousseau's
model can be replicated in modern conditions will be taken up later. Here
it should be noted that Mill's educationally crucial local political level
might give scope for direct participation in decision making.

The stress on local political institutions is not the only extension that
Mill makes to the hypothesis about the educative effect of participation,
but before discussing this other aspect it is useful to note that Mill agrees
with Rousseau about the other two functions of participation. The whole
argument about the 'critical deference' of the multitude rests partly on the
suggestion that participation aids the acceptance of decisions and Mill
specifically points to the integrative function of participation. He says that
through political discussion the individual 'becomes consciously a member
of a great community' (1910, p. 279) and that whenever he has something
to do for the public he is made to feel 'that not only the common weal is
his weal, but that it partly depends on his exertions' (1963, p. 230).

Perhaps the most interesting aspect of Mill's theory is an expansion of
the hypothesis about the educative effect of participation to cover a whole
new area of social life—industry. In his later work, Mill came to see industry as another area where the individual could gain experience in the
management of collective affairs, just as he could in local government. Mill
saw the real value of the various theories of socialism and co-operation
that were being advocated, and sometimes tried out, in his day as lying
in their potential as means of education. As might be expected he was
suspicious of those schemes that were centralist in character; as Robson
points out, Mill in the Chapters on Socialism gives his approval to 'such
socialist schemes as depend on voluntary organisation in small communities and which look to a national application of their principles only
through the self-multiplication of the units' (1968, p. 245). In such a form

of organisation widespread participation could be accommodated. Mill saw co-operative forms of industrial organisation leading to a 'moral transformation' of those that took part in them (he also thought they would be more productive, but that was partly a result of the 'transformation'). A co-operative organisation would lead, he said, to 'friendly rivalry in the pursuit of a good common to all; the elevation of the dignity of labour; a new sense of security and independence in the labouring class; and the conversion of each human being's daily occupation into a school of the social sympathies and the practical intelligence'.[1] Just as participation in the government of the collective interest in local politics educates the individual in social responsibility so participation in the management of the collective interest of an industrial organisation fosters and develops the qualities in the individual that he needs for public activities. 'No soil,' says Mill, could be more conducive to the training of the individual to feel 'the public interest his own' than a 'communist association'.[2] Just as Mill regarded democracy as inevitable in the modern world so he saw some form of co-operation as inevitable in industry; now that the labouring classes had come out of their 'leading strings' the employer/employee relationship would not be maintainable in the long run, some form of co-operation must take its place. In the *Political Economy* Mill discusses what form this might take and he comes to the conclusion that if 'mankind is to continue to improve' then in the end one form of association will predominate, 'not that which can exist between a capitalist as chief, and workpeople without a voice in the management, but the association of the labourers themselves on terms of equality, collectively owning the capital with which they carry on their operations, and working under managers elected and removable by themselves.'[3]

In the same way that participation in local government is a necessary condition for participation at the national level because of its educative or 'improving' effect, so Mill is suggesting that participation in the 'government' of the workplace could have the same impact. These wider implications of Mill's arguments about the importance of education are usually overlooked, yet they are of great significance for democratic theory. If such participation in the workplace is to be possible then the authority relationship in industry would have to be transformed from the usual one of superiority-subordination (managers and men) to one of co-operation or equality with the managers (government) being elected by the whole

[1] Mill (1965), bk. IV, ch. VII, §6, p. 792.
[2] Mill (1965), bk. II, ch. I, §3, p. 205. Mill uses the word 'communist' more loosely than we do today.
[3] Mill (1965), bk. IV, ch. VII, §6, p. 775. See also §§ 2, 3, 4.

body of employees just as representatives at the local level are elected. That is to say, the political relations in industry, using the word 'political' in a wide sense, would have to be democratised. Moreover it is possible to go further; Mill's argument about the educative effect of participation in local government and in the workplace could be generalised to cover the effect of participation in all 'lower level' authority structures, or political systems. It is because this general hypothesis can be derived from their theories that I have referred to these writers as theorists of the participatory society. Society can be seen as being composed of various political systems, the structure of authority of which has an important effect on the psychological qualities and attitudes of the individuals who interact within them; thus, for the operation of a democratic polity at national level, the necessary qualities in individuals can only be developed through the democratisation of authority structures in all political systems.

We might also note at this point that there is another dimension to this theory of participation. Apart from its importance as an educative device, participation in the workplace—a political system—can be regarded as political participation in its own right. Thus industry and other spheres provide alternative areas where the individual can participate in decision making in matters of which he has first hand, everyday experience, so that when we refer to 'participatory democracy' we are indicating something very much wider than a set of 'institutional arrangements' at national level. This wider view of democracy can be found in the political theory of G. D. H. Cole, to which we now turn.

A discussion of Cole's theory—and here we shall be dealing solely with his early writings—is of particular interest because his theory is not only set in the context of a modern, industrialised society but it is very much a theory *of* such a society. The remarks which Mill made about participation in industry, though illuminating for our purposes, were peripheral to his main body of social and political theory, but for Cole it is industry that holds the key that will unlock the door to a truly democratic polity. In his theory of Guild Socialism Cole worked out a detailed scheme of how a participatory society might be organised and brought into being which is of considerable intrinsic interest, although we shall be concerned with the principles that underlay this scheme rather than the blueprint itself. Another significant aspect of Cole's work of this period was the very great influence of Rousseau. There were other influences also, William Morris and Marx, for instance, but Cole frequently quotes Rousseau; the spirit of the latter pervades his work and many of Cole's basic concepts are derived from Rousseau. This is an additional reason for examining Cole's work. Discussions of Rousseau's political theory usually reach the conclusion that it is of little relevance today (and it is sometimes suggested that the influence that it has had has been positively pernicious). I have already argued that Rousseau's theory provides the starting point and the basic material for any discussion of the participatory theory of democracy and Cole's theory provides one attempt to translate the insights of Rousseau's theory into a modern setting.

Cole's social and political theory is built on Rousseau's argument that will, not force, is the basis of social and political organisation. Men must co-operate in associations to satisfy their needs and Cole begins by looking at 'the motives that hold men together in association' and the 'way in which men act through associations in supplement and complement to their actions as isolated or private individuals' (1920, pp. 6 and 11). To translate their will into action in a way that does not infringe upon their individual freedom, Cole argues that men must participate in the organisation and regulation of their associations. The idea of participation is central to his theory. 'I assume', he says, echoing Mill's criticism of Bentham's political theory, 'that the object of social organisation is not merely material efficiency, but also essentially the fullest self-expression of all the members.' Self-expression 'involves self-government' and this means that we must 'call forth the people's full participation in the common direction in the affairs of the community' (1920, p. 208). This, in turn, involves the fullest freedom of all the members for 'freedom is to find perfect expression' (1918, p. 196). Cole also says, again following Rousseau, that the individual is 'most free where he co-operates with his equals in the making of laws'.[1]

Cole's theory is a theory of associations. Society as he defined it is a 'complex of associations held together by the wills of their members'.[2] If the individual is to be self-governing then he not only has to be able to participate in decision making in all the associations of which he is a member but the associations themselves have to be free to control their own affairs (Cole regarded the interference of the state as the main danger here), and if they were to be self-governing in this sense then they have to be roughly equal in political power. In *The World of Labour* Cole

---

[1] Cole (1919, p. 182). But Cole did not accept that freedom consisted in obedience to these laws; he regarded laws as 'the scaffolding of human freedom; but they are not part of the building' (1918, p. 197).

[2] Cole (1920a, p. 12). It should, perhaps, be noted that Cole did not see the whole life of the individual encompassed in these groups. Much of his life, and some of its most valuable aspects, found expression outside association; the individual is 'the pivot on which the whole system of institutions turns. For he alone has in him the various purposes of the various institutions bound together in a single personality'. (1918, p. 191).

argues that the suppression of groups in the French Revolution was an historical accident because of the privileges they then happened to possess, and he adds that 'in recognising that where there must be particular associations, they should be evenly matched, Rousseau admits the group principle to be inevitable in the great state. We may then regard the new philosophy of groups as carrying on the true egalitarian principles of the French Revolution' (1913, p. 23).

This theory of associations is linked to his theory of democracy through the principle of function, 'the underlying principle of social organisation' (1920, p. 48). Cole thought that 'democracy is only real when it is conceived in terms of function and purpose' and the function of an association is based on the purpose for which it was formed (1920a, p. 31). Every association that 'sets before itself any object that is of more than the most rudimentary simplicity finds itself compelled to assign tasks and duties, and with these powers and a share of authority, to some of its members in order that the general object may be effectively pursued' (1920, p. 104). That is, representative government (in the wide sense of that latter term) is necessary in most associations. In Cole's view existing forms of representation are *mis*representation for two reasons. First, because the principle of function has been overlooked, the mistake has been made of assuming that it is possible for an individual to be represented as a whole and for all purposes instead of his being represented in relation to some well-defined function. Second, under the existing parliamentary institutions the elector has no real choice of, or control over, his representative, and the system actually denies the right of the individual to participate because 'having chosen his representative, the ordinary man has, according to that theory, nothing left to do except to let other people govern him'. A system of functional representation, on the other hand, implies 'the constant participation of the ordinary man in the conduct of those parts of the structure of Society with which he is directly concerned, and which he has therefore the best chance of understanding'.[1]

Thus in Cole's theory there is a distinction between the existence of representative 'institutional arrangements' at national level and democracy. For the latter the individual must be able to participate in all the associations with which he is concerned; that is to say, a participatory society is necessary. The democratic principle, Cole says, must be applied 'not only or mainly to some special sphere of social action known as "politics", but to any and every form of social action, and, in especial, to industrial and economic fully as much as to political affairs' (1920a, p. 12). This notion is in fact implicit in Cole's 'new philosophy of groups' that he built on the

[1] Cole (1920, p. 114); see also pp. 104–6.

foundation laid by Rousseau, for it is to apply Rousseau's insights about the functions of participation to the internal organisation of all associations and organisations. For Cole, therefore, like Mill, the educational function of participation is crucial, and he also emphasises that individuals and their institutions cannot be considered in isolation from each other. He remarks in *Guild Socialism Restated* that if Guild Socialist theory was largely a theory of institutions this was not because

it believes that the life of men is comprehended in their social machinery, but because social machinery, as it is good or bad, harmonious or discordant with human desires and instincts, is the means either of furthering, or of thwarting, the expression of human personality. If environment does not, as Robert Owen thought, make character in an absolute sense, it does direct and divert character into divergent forms of expression (1920a, p. 25).

Like Mill, Cole argued that it was only by participation at the local level and in local associations that the individual could 'learn democracy'. 'Over the vast mechanism of modern politics the individual has no control, not because the state is too big, but because he is given no chance of learning the rudiments of self-government within a smaller unit' (1919, p. 157). Actually, Cole has rather disregarded the implications of his own arguments here; the fact that the modern state *is* so big is one important reason for enabling the individual to participate in the 'alternative' political areas of society, a fact that Cole's writings show him to be well aware of.

The important point, however, is that in Cole's view industry provided the all-important arena for the educative effect of participation to take place; for it is in industry that, outside Government, the individual is involved to the greatest extent in relationships of superiority and subordination and the ordinary man spends a great deal of his life at work. It was for this reason that Cole exclaimed that the answer that most people would give to the question 'what is the fundamental evil in our modern society?' would be the wrong one: 'they would answer POVERTY, when they ought to answer SLAVERY' (1919, p. 34). The millions who had been given the franchise, who had formally been given the means to self-government had in fact been 'trained to subservience' and this training had largely taken place during the course of their daily occupation. Cole argued that 'the industrial system . . . is in great measure the key to the paradox of political democracy. Why are the many nominally supreme but actually powerless? Largely because the circumstances of their lives do not accustom or fit them for power or responsibility. A servile system in industry inevitably reflects itself in political servility' (1918, p. 35). Only if the individual could become self-governing in the workplace, only if industry was organised on a participatory basis, could this training for servility be turned into training for democracy and the individual gain the familiarity with democratic procedures, and develop the necessary 'democratic character' for an effective system of large-scale democracy.[1]

For Cole, like Rousseau, there could be no equality of political power without a substantive measure of economic equality and his theory provides us with some interesting indications of how the economic equality in Rousseau's ideal society of peasant proprietors might be achieved in a modern economy. In Cole's view 'the abstract democracy of the ballot box' did not involve real political equality; the equality of citizenship implied by universal suffrage was only formal and it obscured the fact that political power was shared very unequally. 'Theoretical democrats', he said, ignored 'the fact that vast inequalities of wealth and status, resulting in vast inequalities of education, power and control of environment, are necessarily fatal to any real democracy, whether in politics or any other sphere.'[2]

One of Cole's major objections to the capitalist organisation of industry was that under it labour was just another commodity and so the 'humanity' of labour was denied. Under the Guild Socialist system this humanity would be fully recognised, which would mean 'above all else, the recognition of the right . . . to equality of opportunity and status' (1918, p. 24). It is the latter that is really important; only with the equalisation of status could there be the equality of independence that, as we have seen from the discussion of Rousseau's theory, is crucial for the process of participation. Cole thought that there would be a move toward the equalisation of incomes, final equality arising through the 'destruction of the whole idea of remuneration for work done' (1920a, pp. 72–3), but the abolition of status distinctions plays a larger role in his theory. Partly this would come about through the socialisation of the means of production under a Guild Socialist system because classes would then be abolished (by definition—Cole used the term in a Marxian sense), but of more (practical) importance were two other factors. Under a participatory system there would no longer be one group of 'managers' and one group of 'men', the latter having no control over the affairs of the enterprise, but one group of equal decision makers. Secondly, Cole saw a participatory organisation of

[1] Implicit in all Cole's writings on the necessity of a participatory society is the hypothesis that participation will have an integrative effect. This underlies his many references to 'community' and the importance he attaches to local participatory institutions where men can learn the 'social spirit'. In the industrial sphere it is the basis of the assumption that the new form of organisation would lead to co-operation and fellowship in a community of workers instead of the usual industrial conflict. See Cole (1920, p. 169) and (1920a, p. 45).

[2] Cole (1920a, p. 14); see also (1913, p. 421).

industry leading to the abolition of the fear of unemployment for the ordinary man, and so to the abolition of the other great status distinction, inequality in security of tenure of employment.

However, although Cole's democratic theory hinges on the establishment of this equality of status in industry, he was (despite Schumpeter's strictures on this point) very conscious of the problem of the preservation of leadership under such a democratic system, and he thought that the principle of function provided an answer. If representation (leadership) was organised on a functional basis then it was possible to have 'representatives' rather than 'delegates'. The latter seemed necessary because it appeared to be the only way that control could be exercised by the electorate given that 'as soon as the voters have exercised their votes their existence as a group lapses until the time when a new election is required'. Functional associations, by contrast, can have a continuous existence, so can continually advise, criticise and, if necessary, recall the representative. They also have an additional merit in that 'not only will the representative be chosen to do a job about which he knows something, but he will be chosen by persons who know something of it too'.[1]

Although Cole regarded 'material efficiency' as only one object of social and political organisation, he thought that a participatory society would be superior in this respect also. Under conditions of economic security and equality the profit motive—the motive of 'greed and fear'—would be replaced by the motive of free service and workers would see that their efforts were for the benefit of the whole community. He thought that there existed large untapped reserves of energy and initiative in the ordinary man that a participatory system would call forth; it was self-government that was the key to efficiency. The workers would never be persuaded to give of their best 'under a system which from any moral standpoint is utterly indefensible'.[2]

The main interest for our purpose in Cole's specific plan for self-government in the workshop and other spheres, Guild Socialism, is that it provides us with one man's notion, in great detail, of what a participatory society might look like. Cole put forward several versions, but the most theoretically pluralist is to be found in *Guild Socialism Restated* on

---

[1] Cole (1920, pp. 110–13). Such a system would go part of the way to meeting objections often raised about the amount of 'rationality' that a democratic system requires of the voter. Carpenter (1966) has argued that Cole was untouched by the insights of his day into the irrational elements of human behaviour. Be that as it may, Cole like the other theorists of the participatory society took the view that 'rationality' was, at least in part, acquired through the process of participation.

[2] Cole (1919, p. 181) and (1920b, p. 12). Some criticisms of Guild Socialism from an economic point of view can be found in Glass (1966) and Pribicevic (1959).

which this, very brief, account is based.[1] The Guild Socialist structure was organised, vertically and horizontally, from the grass roots upward and was participatory at all levels and in all its aspects. The vertical structure was to be economic in nature—for on good functionalist principles the political and economic functions in society were to be separated. On the economic side production and consumption were also differentiated.[2] What are usually thought of as 'guilds' were actually to be the unit of organisation on the production side. In the economic sphere Cole also proposed the setting up of consumer co-operatives, utility councils (for provision of gas, etc.), civic guilds to take care of health, education, etc., and cultural councils to 'express the civic point of view'—and any other *ad hoc* bodies that might prove necessary in a particular area. The workshop was to be the basic 'building block' of the guild and, similarly, the grass root unit of each council, etc., was to be small enough to allow the maximum participation by everyone. Each guild would elect representatives to the higher stages of the vertical structure, to local and regional guilds and councils, and at the highest level, to the Industrial Guilds Congress (or its equivalent).

The purpose of the horizontal (political) structure was to give expression to 'the communal spirit of the whole society'. Each town or country area would have its own commune where the basic unit would be the ward, again to allow maximum individual participation, and representatives would be elected from the guilds, etc., and any other local bodies to the commune on a ward basis. The next horizontal layer was to be composed of regional communes, bringing together both town and country and the regional guilds, and at the apex would be found the National Commune which would, Cole thought, be a purely co-ordinating body neither functionally, historically nor structurally continuous with the existing state.

The precise merits or demerits of this particular blueprint do not concern us here; as Cole himself said, 'the principles behind guild socialism

---

1 Cole (1920a). An account of the development of Guild Socialism and a general discussion of its theory (Cole was only one of those concerned) can be found in Glass (1966). Whether Cole's plan would have turned out to be as 'pluralist' as he intended has been questioned. He thought that once Guild Socialism began to get under way the state would gradually 'wither away' from lack of a real function, but it has been argued that his National Commune, the new 'co-ordinating' body, would have turned out to be the state renamed in most essentials.

2 It was over this last division that Cole differed both from the collectivists and the advocates of co-operation because neither of these allowed the right of the producer to self-government, and from the syndicalists because they did not admit that consumers needed special representation.

are far more important than the actual forms of organisation which guild socialists have thought out' (1920c, p. 7), and it is with these principles, the principles underlying the theory of participatory democracy, and the question of their empirical relevance at the present time, that we are concerned.

The very great difference between the theories of democracy discussed in this chapter and the theories of those writers whom we have called the theorists of representative government makes it difficult to understand how the myth of one 'classical' theory of democracy has survived so long and is so vigorously propagated. The theories of participatory democracy examined here were not just essays in prescription as is often claimed, rather they offer just those 'plans of action and specific prescriptions' for movement towards a (truly) democratic polity that it has been suggested are lacking. But perhaps the strangest criticism is that these earlier theorists were not, as Berelson puts it, concerned with the 'general features necessary if the (political) institutions are to work as required', and that they ignored the political system as a whole in their work. It is quite clear that this is precisely what they were concerned with. Although the variable identified as crucial in those theories for the successful establishment and maintenance of a democratic political system, the authority structures of non-Governmental spheres of society, is exactly the same one that Eckstein indicates in his theory of stable democracy, the conclusions drawn from this by the earlier and later theorists of democracy are entirely different. In order that an evaluation of these two theories of democracy can be undertaken I shall now briefly set out (in a similar fashion to the contemporary theory of democracy above), a participatory theory of democracy drawn from the three theories just discussed.

The theory of participatory democracy is built round the central assertion that individuals and their institutions cannot be considered in isolation from one another. The existence of representative institutions at national level is not sufficient for democracy; for maximum participation by all the people at that level socialisation, or 'social training', for democracy must take place in other spheres in order that the necessary individual attitudes and psychological qualities can be developed. This development takes place through the process of participation itself. The major function of participation in the theory of participatory democracy is therefore an educative one, educative in the very widest sense, including both the psychological aspect and the gaining of practice in democratic skills and procedures. Thus there is no special problem about the stability of a participatory system; it is self-sustaining through the educative impact of the participatory process. Participation develops and fosters the very qualities necessary for it; the more individuals participate the better able they become to do so. Subsidiary hypotheses about participation are that it has an integrative effect and that it aids the acceptance of collective decisions.

Therefore, for a democratic polity to exist it is necessary for a participatory society to exist, i.e. a society where all political systems have been democratised and socialisation through participation can take place in all areas. The most important area is industry; most individuals spend a great deal of their lifetime at work and the business of the workplace provides an education in the management of collective affairs that it is difficult to parallel elsewhere. The second aspect of the theory of participatory democracy is that spheres such as industry should be seen as political systems in their own right, offering areas of participation additional to the national level. If individuals are to exercise the maximum amount of control over their own lives and environment then authority structures in these areas must be so organised that they can participate in decision making. A further reason for the central place of industry in the theory relates to the substantive measure of economic equality required to give the individual the independence and security necessary for (equal) participation; the democratising of industrial authority structures, abolishing the permanent distinction between 'managers' and 'men' would mean a large step toward meeting this condition.

The contemporary and participatory theories of democracy can be contrasted on every point of substance, including the characterisation of 'democracy' itself and the definition of 'political', which in the participatory theory is not confined to the usual national or local government sphere. Again, in the participatory theory 'participation' refers to (equal) participation in the making of decisions, and 'political equality' refers to equality of power in determining the outcome of decisions, a very different definition from that in the contemporary theory. Finally, the justification for a democratic system in the participatory theory of democracy rests primarily on the human results that accrue from the participatory process. One might characterise the participatory model as one where maximum input (participation) is required and where output includes not just policies (decisions) but also the development of the social and political capacities of each individual, so that there is 'feedback' from output to input.

Many of the criticisms of the so-called 'classical' theory of democracy imply that the latter theory has only to be stated for it to become obvious that it is unrealistic and outmoded. With the participatory theory of democracy this is far from the case; indeed, it has many features that reflect some of the major themes and orientations in recent political

43

theory and political sociology. For example, the fact that it is a model of a self-sustaining system might make it attractive to the many writers on politics who, explicitly or implicitly, make use of such models. Again, similarities between the participatory theory of democracy and recent theories of social pluralism are obvious enough, although these usually argue only that 'secondary' associations should exist to mediate between the individual and the national polity and say nothing about the authority structures of those associations.[1] The wide definition of the 'political' in the participatory theory is also in keeping with the practice in modern political theory and political science. One of the advocates of the contemporary theory of democracy discussed above, Dahl (1963, p. 6), has defined a political system as 'any persistent pattern of human relationships that involves to a significant extent power, rule or authority'. All this makes it very odd that no recent writer on democratic theory appears to have re-read the earlier theorists with these concerns in mind. Any explanation of this would, no doubt, include a mention of the widely held belief that (although these earlier theories are often said to be descriptive) 'traditional' political theorists, especially theorists of democracy, were engaged in a largely prescriptive and 'value-laden' enterprise and their work is thus held to have little direct interest for the modern, scientific, political theorist.

Whatever the truth of that matter, the task that remains, an assessment of the empirical realism and viability of the participatory theory of democracy, can now be undertaken: is the notion of a participatory society utopian fantasy—and dangerous fantasy at that? The exposition of the theory immediately raises several questions of importance. For example, there is the problem of the definition of 'participation'; clearly where direct participation is possible then the definition is relevant but it is not clear, even though the individual would have more opportunities for political participation in a participatory society, how far the paradigm of direct participation can be replicated under conditions where representation is going to be widely necessary. No answer to this question can be attempted, until a good deal of analysis has been undertaken. The theory of participatory democracy stands or falls on two hypotheses: the educative function of participation, and the crucial role of industry, and attention will be concentrated on these. A major point of dispute in the two theories of democracy is whether industrial authority structures can be democratised but before that question can be tackled a more basic question must be asked. In the next chapter we shall begin by seeing if there is any evidence to support the suggested link between participation in the workplace and other non-governmental spheres and participation at the wider, national level.

[1] Cf. Eckstein (1966, p. 191).

CHAPTER III

The sense of political efficacy and participation in the workplace

The contemporary and participatory theories of democracy both include the argument that individuals should receive some 'training' in democracy outside the national political process. However, advocates of the contemporary theory such as Dahl or Eckstein give little indication of how this training takes place, and there is something paradoxical in calling socialisation inside existing organisations and associations, most of which, especially industrial ones, are oligarchical and hierarchical, a training explicitly in *democracy*. The argument in the participatory theory of democracy that the education for democracy that takes place through the participatory process in non-governmental authority structures requires, therefore, that the structures should be democratised, looks, on the face of it, rather more plausible (although Sartori has claimed that it has been disproved that one 'learns to vote by voting'). Before looking to see if there is any empirical evidence to support the suggested connection between participation in the workplace and participation in the wider political sphere, there is a prior question about how this connection might take place. Again, there is common ground here between the two theories as both point to psychological factors as playing the mediating role. The theory of participatory democracy argues that the experience of participation in some way leaves the individual better psychologically equipped to undertake further participation in the future and some interesting evidence in support of this argument can be found in recent empirical studies of political socialisation and political participation.

John Stuart Mill argued that an 'active' character would result from participation, and Cole suggested that what we might call a 'non-servile' character would be fostered, and it is possible to give these notions some useful empirical content. If one is to be self-governing in, for example, one's workplace, then certain psychological qualities are clearly necessary. For example, the belief that one can be self-governing, and confidence in one's ability to participate responsibly and effectively, and to control one's life and environment would certainly seem to be required. These are not characteristics that would be associated with 'servile' or 'passive' characters and it is reasonable to suggest that the acquisition of such confidence, etc., is part, at least, of what the theorists of the participatory society saw as the psychological benefits that would accrue through participation. One could also regard these qualities as being part of the famous 'democratic character'. Now one of the most important positive correlations that has emerged from empirical investigations into political behaviour and attitudes is that between participation and what is known as the sense of political efficacy or sense of political competence. This has been described as the feeling that 'individual political action does have, or can have, an impact upon the political process, i.e. that it is worthwhile to perform one's civic duties' (Campbell *et al.*, 1954, p. 187). People who have a sense of political efficacy are more likely to participate in politics than those in whom this feeling is lacking and it has also been found that underlying the sense of political efficacy is a sense of general, personal effectiveness, which involves self-confidence in one's dealings with the world. 'Persons who feel more effective in their everyday tasks and challenges are more likely to participate in politics',[1] and Almond and Verba have said that 'in many ways . . . the belief in one's competence is a key political attitude' (1965, pp. 206–7). We shall therefore take the sense of political efficacy or competence to be an operational interpretation of, at any rate part of, the psychological effect referred to by the theorists of participatory democracy. The question that now arises is whether there is any evidence to suggest that participation in non-governmental spheres, in particular in industry, is of great importance in the development of this feeling.

The most interesting and important source of evidence is Almond and Verba's book *The Civic Culture*. This is a cross-cultural study of individual political attitudes and behaviour covering five countries, the U.S.A., Great Britain, Germany, Italy and Mexico, and a large part of the book is concerned with the sense of political competence and its development. The authors found that in all five countries a positive relationship held between the sense of political efficacy and political participation, though the sense of competence was higher at local than at national level. It was also found that the level of competence was highest in those countries, the U.S.A. and Britain, where the most institutional opportunities existed for local political participation.[2]

---

[1] Milbrath (1965, p. 59). For a summary of findings relating to political efficacy see Milbrath, pp. 56–60, and Lane (1959), pp. 147 ff.

[2] Almond and Verba (1965, pp. 140 ff., and Tables VI,1 and VI,2).

This gives support to Mill's argument about the importance of local political institutions as a training ground for democracy and, indeed, the authors of the study themselves remark that these facts give one

an argument in favour of the classic position that political participation on the local level plays a major role in the development of a competent citizenry. As many writers have argued, local government may act as a training ground for political competence. Where local government allows participation, it may foster a sense of competence that then spreads to the national level (p. 145).

They also investigated the effects of participation in voluntary organisations and they found that in all five countries the sense of political efficacy was higher among members of organisations than among non-members and highest of all among active members, particularly of explicitly political organisations. We have already noted that the participatory theory of democracy has similarities to recent arguments about social pluralism, and Almond and Verba conclude their chapter on organisational membership by saying that 'pluralism, even if not explicitly political pluralism may indeed be one of the most important foundations of political democracy' (p. 265). In general, recent investigations into political socialisation have shown that the theorists of participatory democracy were on firm ground when they suggested that the individual would generalise from his experiences in non-governmental authority structures to the wider, national political sphere. Like Eckstein in the book considered earlier, Almond and Verba point to these authority structures as the crucial variable involved and they argue that

if in most social situations the individual finds himself subservient to some authority figure, it is likely that he will expect such an authority relationship in the political sphere. On the other hand, if outside the political sphere he has opportunities to participate in a wide range of social decisions, he will probably expect to be able to participate in political decisions as well. Furthermore, participation in non-political decision making may give one the skills needed to engage in political participation (pp. 271-2).

Almond and Verba argue that it is adult experiences that are crucial in this political socialisation process, but more recent research, notably that of Easton (and associates), has focused on the early childhood years as being of fundamental importance in shaping later political behaviour and attitudes. However, although the evidence presented in *Children in the Political System* (Easton and Dennis, 1969) shows that specifically political learning does take place in early childhood, and although it may be true that that learning helps to establish a reservoir of 'diffuse support' for political authority *as such*, the evidence does little, if anything, to establish a connection between specific adult political behaviour or attitudes and the particular kind of childhood learning dealt with in the book (i.e. that the child learns to give meaning to, and to connect with, political authority largely through the personalities of the President and policemen). Indeed, many of the authors' own remarks cast doubt on the later importance of such childhood learning. They note that 'surprisingly, even in an era shot through with Freudian preconceptions, the effect of childhood experiences on adult behaviour is still moot' (p. 75) and that parents tend to shield their children from the realities of political life.[1] It is very significant that the attitudes of the older children differ from those of the younger, under the impact of their increasing (realistic) experience of the world; in fact the authors themselves emphasise the importance of this later experience for political socialisation and say that 'secondary socialisation, during the period beyond childhood, may under certain circumstances work in an opposite direction... with the net outcome dependent on the situational events' (p. 310).

To suggest that we should look to these adult experiences is not to say that childhood is of no importance in political socialisation—later experiences may well reinforce attitudes that began to develop earlier. This point is of direct relevance to the question of the development of the sense of political efficacy among children, which Easton and Dennis have also investigated, but they were not, as were Almond and Verba, concerned with the question of why some individuals feel more politically efficacious than others, but primarily with whether children accept the *norm* of political efficacy. But again this approach tells us nothing about adult political attitudes.[2] The most striking correlation to emerge from studies of political efficacy is that different levels are linked to socioeconomic status; low SES individuals tend to be low in a sense of political efficacy (and to participate less). This correlation between class and levels of efficacy also holds for children, and Easton and Dennis argue that the levels of efficacy measured in children in fact reflect the child's view of parents' attitudes and behaviour (1967, p. 31). This being so, then we still have to account for the difference in adults in this respect and it will not do merely to say that this is a result of *their* own childhood ...

The area where such an explanation may be found has already been

[1] Pp. 357–8. See also Greenstein (1965, p. 45) and Orren and Peterson (1967). Easton's and Dennis's findings are also probably culture-bound, a fact that they themselves recognise (see e.g. Jaros *et al.*, 1968).

[2] It is a curious argument (Easton and Dennis, 1967, p. 38) that the 'internalisation' early in life of a norm that one ought to have a say in government will, in itself, help to counteract later frustration when we find that apparent opportunities to do so are illusory. It would seem more likely that it would have the opposite effect.

indicated—in the individual's experiences of non-governmental authority structures, and this can provide us with an explanation of both childhood and adult differences. Almond and Verba found that (remembered) opportunities to participate in the family and at school did correlate with a high score on the political competence scale in all five countries, the impact of opportunities at the higher educational level being of particular importance. It is middle-class children who are most likely to score high on the efficacy scale and we know that middle-class families are most likely to provide their children with a 'participatory' family authority structure, working-class families tending to be more 'authoritarian' or to exhibit no consistent pattern of authority. Since middle-class children are also more likely to go on to higher education, we begin to see the appearance of a cumulative pattern of participation opportunities.[1]

However, despite these differences already apparent in childhood, it is Almond and Verba's view that adult experiences are crucial. On the basis of data from five different countries they conclude that 'in a relatively modern and diversified social system socialisation in the family and, to a lesser extent, in the school represents inadequate training for political participation' (p. 305). Of 'crucial significance' for the development of the sense of political efficacy are opportunities to 'participate in decisions at one's place of work. The structure of authority at the workplace is probably the most significant—and salient—structure of that kind with which the average man finds himself in daily contact' (p. 294).

In fact experiences with different kinds of authority structures at the workplace on the part of adults can also provide us with an explanation of the differing levels of political efficacy found in their children. One explanation offered for the class difference in child-rearing is the effect of low-status occupations on fathers; 'fathers whose work gives them little autonomy, and who are controlled by others, exercising no control themselves, are found to be more aggressive and severe' (Cotgrove 1967, p. 57), i.e. they do not provide a participatory home environment.

---

[1] Almond and Verba, pp. 284 ff., Tables XI. 4 and XI. 5. Easton and Dennis (1967) and Greenstein (1965, pp. 90 ff.). For a convenient account of class differences in child-rearing patterns in England see Klein (1965), vol. II. Another significant factor is that secondary-modern schools, attended by most lower SES children, often operated by what have been called 'drill sergeant' methods, allowing little room for the child to make decisions in any respect. For a model of this type of school see Webb (1962). It is interesting that in Norway the difference in the levels of political efficacy between classes is less than in the U.S.A. and one explanation offered is in terms of the different structure of the political parties; in Norway they are 'class-polarised' and hence provide a greater number of opportunities for lower SES persons to participate. See Rokkan and Campbell (1960) and Alford (1964).

Certainly, experiences at work do affect the development of a sense of political efficacy in adults. Almond and Verba asked respondents whether they were consulted about decisions made on the job, the extent to which they felt free to complain about decisions and the extent to which they actually complained. In all countries opportunities to participate were positively correlated to a feeling of political competence, and also, as one might expect, the higher the status of the respondent the more opportunities were reported.[1]

It was also found that participation was cumulative in effect; the more areas in which an individual participated the higher his score on the political efficacy scale was likely to be.[2] We have already noted that such a cumulation of participation opportunities is most likely to occur for higher SES individuals. It is the lower SES group that in the general run of things have the least opportunities for participation, particularly in the workplace. It is almost part of the definition of a low status occupation that the individual has little scope for the exercise of initiative or control over his job and working conditions, plays no part in decision making in the enterprise and is told what to do by his organisational superiors. This situation would lead to feelings of ineffectiveness that would be reinforced by lack of opportunities to participate, that would lead to feelings of ineffectiveness . . . and so on. An effect of this kind was emphasised some years ago in an article by Knupfer called *Portrait of the Underdog*. There it was argued that the different aspects of status cluster together and take on the aspect of a vicious circle that 'recalls the Biblical dictum "to him that hath shall be given" '. The author emphasises the importance of psychological factors in this process and suggests that the commonly found lack of effort to control their environment by lower SES groups may arise from 'deeply ingrained habits of doing what one is told'. Economic underprivilege is thus linked to *psychological* underprivilege and engenders 'a lack of self confidence which increases the unwillingness of the lower status person to participate in many phases of our predominantly middle class culture beyond what would be a realistic withdrawal adapted to the reduced chances of being effective'. (1954, p. 263).

Evidence has now been presented to support the argument of the theory of participatory democracy that participation in non-governmental authority structures is necessary to foster and develop the psychological qualities (the sense of political efficacy) required for participation at the national level. Evidence has also been cited to support the argument that industry is

[1] Almond and Verba (1965), pp. 280–3, Table XI. 3, and pp. 294–7, Table XI. 6.
[2] Almond and Verba, pp. 297–99, Tables XI. 7 and XI. 8. This finding did not hold for Mexico.

the most important sphere for this participation to take place and this does give us the basis for a possible explanation of why it is that low levels of efficacy are more likely to be found among lower SES groups. We shall now examine some further empirical evidence on the effect that different types of industrial authority structure have on the attitudes and outlook of individuals.

Recently there has been considerable interest in the effect that different types of authority structure and different technologies have on those that work within them. Just as a low status worker is, in an hierarchical authority structure, in the position of permanent subordinate, so, in some technologies he can be subordinated also to the, external, demands of the technical process.[1] An interesting illustration of this can be found in Blauner's comparative study of four different work situations. In *Alienation and Freedom* (1964) Blauner looked at the (American) printing, textile, automobile and chemical industries, where the rank and file worker's relation to the division of labour, the organisation of the work and the technical process varied greatly, as did the impact of these factors on the worker. Only certain work situations were found to be conducive to the development of the psychological characteristics in which we are interested, the feelings of personal confidence and efficacy that underly the sense of political efficacy. These conditions were not present in the automobile or textile industries. In the former, 'the automobile work environment is so highly rationalised that workers have practically no opportunity to solve problems and contribute their own ideas' and on the line itself the worker has no control over the pace or technique of his work, no room to exercise skill or leadership (pp. 98 and 111–13). This technology, together with the characteristic authority structure of an automobile assembly plant, contribute little to the individual's sense of self-esteem and the 'social personality of the auto worker . . . is expressed in a characteristic

[1] The effect that certain types of industrial processes had on those employed in them was noted by Adam Smith: he wrote, 'in the progress of the division of labour, the employment . . . of the great body of the people comes to be confined to a few simple operations; frequently to one or two. But the understandings of the greater part of men are necessarily formed by their ordinary employments. The man whose whole life is spent in performing a few simple operations of which the effects too are, perhaps, always the same . . . has no occasion to exert his understanding or to exercise his invention in finding out expedients for removing difficulties which never occur. He naturally loses, therefore, the habit of such exertion and generally becomes as stupid and ignorant as it is possible for a human creature to become . . . [he in incapable] of forming any just judgement concerning many even of the ordinary duties of private life. Of the great and extensive interests of his country, he is altogether incapable of judging'. Smith (1880), vol. II, pp. 365–6.

attitude of cynicism toward authority and institutional systems' (p. 178). The situation in the textile industry was even less conducive to the development of feelings of personal efficacy. Here, not only did the technical process reduce the worker's control over his job to a minimum but he was also 'at the mercy of both major and minor supervisors'. Blauner quotes from a psychological study that was made of the textile workers and it described the typical personality of a mill-worker as being one where he is 'resigned to his lot ... more dependent than independent ... he lacks confidence in himself ... he is humble ... the most prevalant feeling states ... seem to be fear and anxiety' (pp. 69–70 and 80). The contrast between these two industries and the printing and chemical industries was marked. In the printing industry, still largely a craft industry, the worker has a high degree of personal control over his work, has high, internalised standards of workmanship and responsibility and a very large degree of freedom from external control. All these factors add up, says Blauner to a 'social personality characterised by ... a strong sense of individualism and autonomy, and a solid acceptance of citizenship in the larger society. [The printer] ... has a highly developed feeling of self-esteem and a sense of self-worth and is therefore ready to participate in the social and political institutions of the community' (pp. 176 and 43 ff.). A similar result is found in the chemical industry, but there, not because of the high degree of control over job and conditions exercised by an individual craftsman, but through the collective responsibility of a crew of employees for the maintenance and smooth working of a continuous process plant. Each crew had control over the pace and method of getting the work done, and the work crews were largely internally self-disciplining. As with the printing industry this work situation contributed to self-esteem and self-worth (pp. 132 ff., 179 and 159). Blauner concluded that the 'nature of a man's work affects his social character and personality' and that an 'industrial environment tends to breed a distinct social type.'[1]

The impact of hierarchical authority structures and the sub-division of work on personality has also received attention from writers on organisation and management and they approach the question from the point of view of the efficiency of the organisation. For this, it is typically argued, is needed an authority structure and work organisation that does not impair the 'mental health', the psychological efficiency, of the employee. Argyris, for example, on the basis of two models, one of the hierarchical (bureaucratic) organisation, and the other of the psychologically healthy individual has argued that the typical form of authority structure in modern industry

---

[1] Blauner (1964), pp. VIII and 166. Similar evidence of the effect of different work environments on political attitudes can be found in Lipsitz (1964).

fails to meet individual needs for self-esteem, self-confidence and growth and so forth and he cites copious empirical material in support of this argument. This does not affect only those at the bottom of the structure. The 'organisational norms', Argyris argues, force the executive to hide his feelings and this makes it difficult for him to develop the competence and confidence in interpersonal relationships on which efficient management depends and makes him unwilling to take risks. This, in turn, tends to increase the 'rigidity' in the organisation which reinforces its deleterious effects on the rank and file.[1] Typically, the rank and file worker in modern industry finds himself in a work environment where he can use few abilities, and exercises little or no initiative or control over his work. This may result in him experiencing 'a decreasing sense of self-control and self-responsibility' and the cumulative effect over a period may be to 'influence the employee's view of himself, his esteem of himself . . . his satisfaction in his life, and indeed his values about the meaning of work'. Aygyris does speculate that these psychological states may be linked to a lack of interest and activity in politics but he does not investigate this aspect himself (1964, pp. 54 and 87–8).

It seems clear from this evidence that the argument of the participatory theory of democracy that an individual's (politically relevant) attitudes will depend to a large extent on the authority structure of his work environment is a well-founded one. Specifically, the development of a sense of political efficacy does appear to depend on whether his work situation allows him any scope to participate in decision making. This being so, then the crucial question so far as the general empirical validity of the theory of participatory democracy is concerned, is how far it is in fact possible for industry to be organised on participatory lines. It is with this question that we shall be dealing from this point.

There is a considerable body of evidence available from different sources on industrial democracy and participation in the workplace, indeed, the term 'participation' has enjoyed something of a vogue among writers on management and allied topics over the past few years. But none of this material has been considered by the advocates of the contemporary theory of democracy, not even by Eckstein who has argued that it is not possible to democratise industrial authority structures. So far in our

---

[1] Argyris (1957) and (1964). This is, of course, a similar argument to that of Merton in his well-known essay on *Bureaucratic Structure and Personality* where he says that with bureaucratic organisational forms increasing 'it becomes plain to all who would see that man is to a very important degree controlled by his social relation to the instruments of production. This can no longer seem only a tenet of Marxism but a stubborn fact to be acknowledged by all'. This leads, he argues, to displacement of goals, timidity, ritualism, impersonality and so on. Merton (1957).

discussion of the theory of participatory democracy we have used the terms 'participation' and 'democracy' as virtually synonymous and this is how they are used in the bulk of the managerial literature that we shall review. This usage is mistaken, but the question of the precise relationship between the two, or rather that between industrial democracy and the different forms that participation can take, must be left until the empirical material has been examined; in fact the relationship is considerably more complicated than is often supposed. Another, related, problem that will also be considered is how the psychological effects of participation in the workplace relate to the different forms of participation and to industrial democracy.

Before the examination of the empirical material begins it will be useful to consider briefly an argument that would make the whole undertaking irrelevant. Although participation in the workplace has been shown to be important for wider political participation it could be argued that, nevertheless, it is not of central importance because today, and increasingly, leisure is the most important part of the worker's life and the sphere where he expects to gain, and can gain, psychological satisfactions. Writers who argue for the central importance of leisure in the life of today's rank and file worker point to the fact that many, particularly manual workers, are tending to regard work as something having purely instrumental value and centring their aspirations on leisure. Thus, one could, by extending this argument, suggest that leisure might provide a replacement for work so far as the development of the sense of political efficacy is concerned.[1] However, there are considerable difficulties with this argument.

Firstly, even if work could replace lesiure in this respect, it would result, as Blauner (1964) pointed out, in a basic inequity, 'a division of society

[1] From the point of view of the participatory theory of democracy such an instrumental attitude could be taken as an indication that the worker was not operating in a participatory environment. The latter would be expected to lead to an evaluation of work in terms of intrinsic factors because of the psychological benefits attainable. In the quotation from Argyris, above, it was suggested that certain types of work environment could lead the worker to re-evaluate work itself, and similar arguments about the work situation leading to the re-evaluation of work on instrumental lines can be found in e.g. Chinoy (1955) and Lipsitz (1964). In the recent book on the Vauxhall car workers it is argued that an instrumental attitude is brought to the job rather than being developed there. However, the points made about the increasing social pressures on the individual worker to regard his work in an instrumental light are not incompatible with the work-situation thesis. The authors do not consider the impact of the authority structure of the car plant nor offer any evidence whether attitudes to work had changed while the workers were at Vauxhalls. Goldthorpe et al. (1968).

into one segment of consumers who are creative in their leisure time but have meaningless work and a second segment capable of self-realisation in both spheres of life' (p. 184). But this presupposes that the same, or equivalent psychological benefits accrue in both leisure and work, yet there are significant differences between them. The term 'leisure' covers a wide range of activities, some of which, especially some hobbies, do closely resemble 'work' activities, but they differ in the context in which they are carried on. By 'work' we mean not just the activity that provides for most people the major determinant of their status in the world, or the occupation that the individual follows 'full time' and that provides him with his livelihood, but we refer also to activities that are carried on in co-operation with others, that are 'public' and intimately related to the wider society and its (economic) needs; thus we refer to activities that, potentially, involve the individual in decisions about collective affairs, the affairs of the enterprise and of the community, in a way that leisure-time activities most usually do not. But even if some hobbies might have the same psychological effects as Blauner indicates accrue to the (printer) craftsman, all leisure activities are not hobbies, many—most—do not involve the production of anything by the individual, rather he consumes, so that the activity as well as the context is different. More importantly the 'leisure argument' ignores the assertion of the theorists of the participatory society of the interrelationship of individuals and institutions; if a certain kind of industrial authority structure can affect political participation then might it not affect leisure as well? This kind of link has been suggested by several writers. For example, Bell (1960), who writes that ' "conspicuous loafing" is the hostile gesture of a tired working class' (p. 233), and Friedman (1961), who argues that 'fragmentation of labour does not always cause the worker to seek leisure activities of greater scope in order to compensate for his frustrations. It may tend instead to disorganise the rest of his life' (p. 113), and who regards 'killing time' as a general feature of mass behaviour at the present time. Riesman has changed his mind about what he wrote on leisure in The Lonely Crowd and more recently has argued that both work and leisure must be 'meaningful'.[1] Finally, to add force to arguments on these lines there is the significant fact that those persons who participate most in 'public' types of leisure activities (voluntary organisations, politics) are just those groups, the upper SES groups, that are most likely to work in an environment conducive to the development of a sense of personal efficacy. But even if the leisure argument looked more plausible most people, at least in Britain, have very little leisure time and it appears that for the foreseeable

[1] Riesman (1956 and 1964). See also Mills (1963).

future work will still occupy a large slice of most people's waking hours.[1]

As with many words which attain a measure of popularity in a particular context, the term 'participation' has been used by writers on different aspects of industry and management in various senses without these being made at all clear, or, indeed, without the writers themselves giving any indication that they are aware that several senses are involved. From our examination of the empirical evidence on industrial participation we shall distinguish three main senses, or forms of participation. The evidence will also enable something to be said about the specific hypotheses about the effects of participation advanced by the theorists of participatory democracy and about its effects on the economic efficiency of the enterprise.

In the evidence quoted from Blauner's book on the impact of different work situations on individual's psychological orientations the crucial variable was the amount of control that the individual was able to exercise over his job and job environment. In the discussion of Rousseau's theory of participation the close connection between control and participation in decision making was emphasised and it is fairly obvious that if an individual is to exercise such control then he will have to participate in at least those decisions that directly affect his particular job. There is, at present, a widespread desire among many different categories of worker for such participation. In a survey carried out in Norway covering over 1,100 non-supervisory workers in Oslo, 56% of the blue collar workers and 67% of the white collar felt that they would like to participate more in 'decisions that directly concerned my own work and working conditions'.[2] In a study of 5,700 American workers in heavy industry it was found that over half wanted more say in the way in which the work was carried out.[3] In Britain, there is some indirect evidence on this topic from the trend which strikes have taken since the war. Strikes over other than wage demands, particularly strikes relating to working arrangements, rules and discipline, now total about three-quarters of all stoppages; that is, most strikes are now over issues that, broadly, relate to 'control'. Turner has commented that it could be said that these strikes all 'involve attempts to submit managerial discretion and authority to agreed ... rules; alternatively that they reflect an implicit pressure for more democracy and individual rights in industry' (Turner, 1963, p. 18).

The same desire can be seen reflected in the (voluminous) material on job satisfaction. It might be supposed that most workers would be dissatisfied with jobs that allowed them to exercise very little control, but in

---

[1] See Boston (1968). The speed at which automation will be introduced has also often been overestimated, e.g. see Blumberg (1968, p. 55).

[2] Holter (1965, p. 301, Table 2).   [3] Cited in Blumberg (1968, p. 115).

fact just the opposite appears to be the case; all the evidence shows that most workers are satisfied with their jobs. This evidence of general satisfaction is now being interpreted rather more cautiously than it often was in the past. As Goldthorpe has recently remarked, 'results of this kind have in fact been several times achieved in cases where other evidence has indicated fairly clearly that the workers in question experienced quite severe deprivations in performing their jobs'.[1] More significant are the reasons given for *disliking* a job; the main one is that the individual can exercise very little control over what he does or the conditions under which he does it. This applies particularly to the most extreme case (as we have seen from Blauner's study) of the 'man on the track'. Those assembly line workers who do find the job satisfactory often give as a reason that they are able to build up banks of work, i.e. they find a way to exercise a bit of control. In general it is found that satisfaction expressed with a job declines as skill level declines, and the least skilled jobs would be the least likely to involve much opportunity for controlling the work process.[2] Blauner (1960, p. 353) has remarked that 'the fact that surrender of such control seems to be the most important condition of strong dissatisfaction [is a finding] at least as important as the overall one of general satisfaction'.

So much research has been carried out on job satisfaction and its relationship to the worker's desire for more control (participation) over his immediate work and environment because the worker's satisfaction with his job has been found to be closely related to his morale and to his efficiency and productivity. An increase in his satisfaction has a beneficial effect on a whole host of other factors from the point of view of both the worker and the enterprise as a whole, thus various practical attempts have been made to combat the psychological effects of the extreme sub-

---

[1] Goldthorpe *et al.* (1968, p. 11). There are various reasons for this odd fact. Work meets a whole multitude of human needs including those for sheer activity and social intercourse; it is also difficult for a worker to admit he dislikes his job and not threaten his self-respect, he is 'condemned out of his own mouth for not bestirring himself to find more congenial work' (Flanders *et al.*, 1968, pp. 120–1; see also Blauner, 1960). One also finds workers making comments like 'if I didn't enjoy [work] I would be miserable' (Zwieg, 1961, p. 77). The latter provides also an example of the uncritical interpretation of the 'satisfaction' finding when he says 'the syndrome "Unhappy Worker" may have been a fact in the past . . . but there is very little of it in modern, well-organised and well-run industrial establishments' (p. 79). An interesting theory about job satisfaction which throws light on these findings can be found in Hertzberg (1959) and (1968).

[2] This last finding holds for the U.S.S.R. as well; see Hertzberg (1959, pp. 164–5). On the assembly line worker see Walker and Guest (1952, pp. 58 ff.) and the comments in Goldthorpe *et al.* (1968, p. 23).

division of labour. One of these is the idea of job enlargement. A job is 'enlarged' when its content is increased and, according to a management specialist, there are three major assumptions behind this idea: it will enable the worker to use more of his abilities, give him more control, and so increase output; secondly, it will create greater interest and so increase satisfaction and finally it will help overcome 'the inability to secure from the rank and file any real feeling of participation in the affairs of a business or enduring concern for its success' (Stephens, 1962). A typical example of job enlargement is provided by the reorganisation of the jobs of girls on an assembly line so that they performed nine operations instead of just one, did their own inspection, and obtained some of their own supplies.[1]

Job enlargement can be seen as a rudimentary example of one form of, or as a step towards, participation in the workplace. In fact, the larger job enlargement experiments are almost indistinguishable in form from the more minor examples of experiments that are explicitly labelled 'participation' experiments and this is because the same hypothesis about the amount of control that the individual can exercise over his work and his psychological attitude underlies both. Various 'participation' experiments have been carried out over the past two decades, both as a result of deliberate management policy and as a result of initiatives from the workers concerned, and the accounts of these experiments, previously rather inaccessible, have now been gathered together and summarised by Blumberg in Chapter 5 of his recent book *Industrial Democracy: The Sociology of Participation* (1968). As he points out, these participation experiments have taken place in a wide variety of organisational settings

including boys' clubs, women's organisations, college classrooms, factories of many different kinds, offices, stores, scientific laboratories, and so on. Similarly, they have been conducted upon a tremendous variety of persons differing in age, sex, education, income, occupation, and power. They have involved young boys, housewives, college students, manual workers at different levels of skill and in diverse types of factories, supervisors at different levels, clerical workers, salesmen, and scientists (p. 73).

In the industrial participation experiments an increase in worker participation has invariably been found to have beneficial results. For instance, in one of the best known, four groups of workers were selected in a garment factory. In two, all the members participated in the reorganisation of their job on the basis of a plan presented by the management. In another group they participated through representatives and in the fourth no participation at all occurred. The result was that in the latter group there was

[1] Guest (1962). Stephens (1962) provides several varied examples; see also Blumberg (1968), pp. 66–8; Friedman (1961), ch. IV; and Walker (1962), pt. 2, §4.

hostility, a fall in output and some workers left. In the two 'total participation' groups, in contrast, the atmosphere was co-operative and production increased.[1] The common feature of all the experiments cited
by Blumberg is that they enabled workers to decide for themselves
matters previously reserved for a unilateral management decision, matters
such as the speed of work, the allocation of work, how a change in the
job is to be organised and so on. The important thing is the psychological
effect that this participation had on the participants; in effect, in these
experiments the worker's position was transformed into one analogous to
that of the craftsman as described by Blauner, so that as well as an increase
in his satisfaction with the job one would expect his sense of personal
confidence and competence to increase also, and this is, in fact, the case.
Thus, these experiments provide further empirical confirmation of the
contention of the theorists of participatory democracy of the importance
of the interaction between the psychological orientations of individuals
and the authority structure of their institutions.

However, although the examples in Blumberg's book do involve an
increase in participation in decision making by workers, they are all
examples of rather small, short-term experiments, involving few workers
and relatively minor decisions, and, more importantly, the overall structure of authority in the enterprise is hardly affected at all. A major
defect of Blumberg's book is that though he has conveniently collected
together these examples of experiments in participation, he has not set
these within the context of an analysis of the concept of (industrial)
participation itself and so does not discriminate sufficiently between the
various examples nor systematically relate the small-scale participation
experiments to his discussion of participation on a very much larger
scale in the chapter devoted to the organisation of industry in Yugoslavia.
He has also overlooked some important material on industrial participation which provides an example of a different form of participation from
that in the participation experiments material. The latter provides an
example of what we shall call 'partial participation' but there is also
evidence available which illustrates that what we shall call 'full participation' is possible. The significant difference is that in the latter situation
groups of workers are largely self-disciplining and a considerable transformation of the authority structure of the enterprise takes place, at least
at the level of the everyday work process. Moreover, in the examples that
follow, not only do groups of workers exercise full control over their
work over a wide area, but they do so not as part of an experiment but in
the course of their day-to-day work; indeed, their work is organised on

[1] Coch and French (1948). See Blumberg (1968, pp. 80–4).

precisely that basis. These examples are also of interest for a quite different reason. If a necessary condition for democracy is a participatory society, most importantly a participatory industrial sphere, then the problem arises of how the transition is to be made to a system of this kind, for clearly the sort of examples of participation mentioned so far fall far short of what is required by the theory of participatory democracy. Cole, in fact, had an answer to this problem; he saw the transition coming about through a policy of 'encroaching control'. This policy was directed 'not to the admission of the workers to the conjoint exercise of a common control with the employer but to the transference of certain functions *completely* from the employer to the workers' (1920b, p. 156). The means through which this transfer would take place was the collective contract; collective bargaining would be extended over a much wider field than at present and give the workers new powers. A contract would be negotiated by all the workers in a particular shop or enterprise under which the workers collectively would control such matters as hiring and firing, pace of output and choice of foreman, and they would, as a group, be responsible for discipline and would receive a lump (collective) payment which would be shared out by the men in an agreed distribution.[1] That this sort of arrangement and this sort of participation by workers is quite feasible is shown by examples drawn from two very different industries.

Collective arrangements have been a traditional feature of British mining, and the modern form, in the Durham coalfields, has been the subject of intensive and detailed study in recent years, the study initially being prompted by the large amount of stress illness to be found among miners.[2] Under the traditional working methods the miner, the collier, supervised himself and was directly responsible for production; the role of the deputy was one of service rather than supervision. Post-war, a form of work organisation had been adopted, known as conventional longwall working, that was based on mass production methods and the division of labour. It was from this form of work organisation that the investigators saw the deleterious psychological effects arising. In particular, this method

[1] See e.g. Cole (1920b, pp. 154–7) and (1920a, pp. 198 ff.).
[2] The work was carried out by the Tavistock Institute of Human Relations within the framework of a concept developed by them, that of the 'socio-technical system'. The relevance of this concept to the present discussion is obvious; from this viewpoint a productive system is seen not just in terms of a technological process, but as a system of three interrelated variables, the technological, the economic and the socio-psychological. The form of work-organisation and its social and psychological properties are seen as independent of, though limited by, the technology. See e.g. Trist and Emery (1962).

meant that co-ordination and control had to be provided externally, by the management, and this implied a degree of coercion that was completely out of place in a high-risk situation.[1] But there was also another form of work organisation available, one that had its roots in the traditional mining methods, the composite longwall method; this involved a form of collective contract and the abolition of the rigid division of labour, the workers operating as a self-regulating group. This has been described as follows:

> The group takes over complete responsibility for the total cycle of operations involved in mining at the coal face. No member of the group has a fixed work role. Instead, the men deploy themselves, depending on the requirements of the on-going group task. Within the limits of technology and safety requirements they are free to evolve their own way of organising and carrying out their task. They are not subject to any external authority in this respect, nor is there within the group itself any member who takes over a formal directive leadership function . . . The all-in wage agreement is . . . based on the negotiated price per ton of coal produced by the team. The income obtained is divided equally among the team members (Herbst, 1962, p. 4).

Under the composite longwall system productivity was higher than under the conventional longwall method and it was more conducive to 'low cost, work satisfaction, good relations and social health' (Trist et al., 1963, p. 291). For two years, groups of forty to fifty miners operated in this way and at the end of that time were, in the opinion of the investigators still growing 'in their capacity to adapt to changes in their task environment and to satisfy the needs of their members'.[2]

Again, it is the psychological impact of the wide-ranging participation in decision making that such a collective contract makes possible that is important. But if miners, and mining, might be thought to be in some sense exceptional, there is a second example of this form of participation to be found in the car industry. In his book *Decision-making and Productivity* (1958), Melman gives an account of the gang system of work organisation that operated at the Standard car plant at Coventry in the early 1950s. Although the tasks that each worker performed were very much the same as at any other car assembly plant the form of work organisation was quite different, being based on self-regulating groups similar to those

---

[1] Trist and Bamforth (1951) and Trist et al. (1963, pp. 289 ff.).

[2] Trist et al. (1963, p. xiii). An experiment in the reorganisation of work in a textile mill in India using self-regulating groups of workers was also successfully carried out. See Rice (1958). J. S. Mill also mentions a collective contract among Cornish miners of his time and noted that this system produced 'a degree of intelligence, independence and moral elevation, which raises the condition and character of the Cornish miner far above that of the generality of the labouring class'. Mill (1965), bk. iv, ch. vii, §5, p. 769.

in the composite longwall method of mining. (Hence the name 'gang system'.) In 1953 in the motor vehicle plant the workers were grouped into fifteen self-recruiting gangs, and in the tractor plant all 3,000 workers operated as one gang, payment being on the basis of the occupational rate plus a bonus based on gang output as a whole. Under this system the workers 'are not only production employees carrying out . . . occupational tasks. They are also active as formulators of decisions on production which they themselves execute' (1958, p. 92). A car worker describing the gang system said that it 'provides a natural frame of security, it gives confidence, shares money equally, uses all degrees of skill without distinction and enables jobs to be allocated to the man or woman best suited to them, the allocation frequently being made by the workers themselves' (Wright, 1961, p. 50). Melman concluded that under the gang system 'thousands of workers operated virtually without supervision, as conventionally understood, and at high productivity; the highest wage in British industry was paid; high quality products were produced at acceptable prices in extensively mechanised plants; the management conducted its affairs at unusually low costs; also workers had a substantial role in production decision making' (1958, p. 5).

Melman does not specifically consider the psychological effect of the gang system, but in the light of the evidence from the mining industry, and from the fact that this sort of collective self-regulation is analogous to the situation of the crews in the chemical plant described by Blauner, it can be concluded that it would be conducive to the development of the sense of efficacy and competence in which we are interested. It is very significant that the situation in the car industry can be transformed in this way, for we have already seen that within an orthodox authority structure it has precisely the opposite psychological effect; these two examples show that it is possible, at least at the level of the everyday work process, for the authority structure in industry to be considerably modified, for workers to exercise almost complete control over their jobs and to participate in a wide range of decision making, without any loss in productive efficiency.

Finally, there is a large body of material of direct relevance to participation in the workplace in the form of experiments on the effects of different styles of supervision, and what might be called (following Likert) theories about new patterns of management. It is within this context that the notion of 'participation' has recently become so popular, though, curiously enough, the form that the participation takes here often involves no decision making at all and is what we shall later distinguish as 'pseudo participation'. The real interest of this material, apart from giving further confirmation to points already made, lies in the light that it throws onto the specific hypotheses about participation put forward by the theorists of participatory democracy, and secondly, that it is influential in actual management practice today.

In the late 1930s a very famous series of small-group experiments was undertaken under the direction of Lewin, that seemed to show that a 'democratic' form of leadership was more effective than either an 'authoritarian' or 'laissez faire' form. The superiority arose from the psychological effects of the element of participation that the 'democratic' form allowed, and this enhanced the morale of the group, their satisfaction with, and interest in, the task, etc.[1] The more recent experiments on supervisory styles grew out of these earlier ones and accounts of these, and their effects, can be found in the book by Blumberg referred to above (1968, pp. 102–19). Usually, 'close' and 'general' or 'participatory' styles are contrasted. The latter seems to be related 'to a whole cluster of other traits, such as tendencies to delegate authority, not to impose pressure on subordinates, and to permit freedom of conduct to employees . . . under general supervision workers are freer to use their own initiative, to make more decisions concerning their job, and to implement these decisions' (Blumberg, p. 103). This style of supervision gives rise to a situation similar to that created by job enlargement or the participation experiments and the psychological effects and the favourable effect on efficiency are also similar.

The enhanced group harmony and sense of co-operation that the experience of participation invariably gives rise to supports the suggestion of the theorists of participatory democracy that participation has an integrative function; the emphasis placed on results of this kind in the participation literature also supports the suggestion that participation aids the acceptance of decisions. The small group experiments add some interesting evidence on this point. In the participation experiment briefly described earlier on pp. 58–9, the point of the exercise was to find the best method to ensure the smooth introduction of a change into the work process. In fact, one of the main hypotheses that small-group experiments have been used to test is what Verba (1961) calls the 'participation hypothesis', viz. that 'significant changes in human behaviour can be brought about rapidly only if the persons who are expected to change participate in deciding what the change shall be and how it shall be made' (p. 206). In the discussion of Rousseau's theory it was noted that part of the reason that the individual found a law made through the participatory process acceptable was that it was 'impersonal' (it left the individual 'his

[1] There are various accounts of these experiments. See e.g. White and Lippitt (1960).

own master'). In the small-group experiments each individual, during the decision-making process, was able to observe the others accepting the decision and so make an 'internalised' commitment to it himself, and Verba cites several experiments that indicated that the 'impersonality' of such decisions is a major factor in making them acceptable.[1] This supervisory and small-group material also provides some evidence, though not as much as one would like, on another aspect of the theory of participatory democracy. The advocates of the contemporary theory argue that certain personality traits (the 'authoritarian' or 'non-democratic' character) have to be taken as given—the active participation of such individuals would be dangerous for the democratic political system. The participatory theory, on the other hand, argues that the experience of participation itself will develop and foster the 'democratic' personality, i.e. qualities needed for the successful operation of the democratic system, and will do so for all individuals. Blumberg (1968) points out that the early Lewin experiments showed that 'personality traits . . . were dependent variables, significantly altered by the organisation of the group into authoritarian, democratic, or laissez-faire structures' (p. 109). Another study found that where workers employed in routine clerical work operated for a year in a participatory situation, this resulted in a decrease in the potency of 'hierarchical trends' in their personalities and the 'autonomous trends' had more opportunity for expression; 'the data seem to indicate that measurable change can be affected by a persisting change in environmental conditions. Furthermore, the change seems partly explicable in terms of the movement of personality toward equilibrium with its environment' (Tannenbaum, 1957). Or, as Blumberg puts it 'a structure of participation . . . in the long run becomes more effective because of the eventual compatibility of personality with structure. In other words, the organisation that permits participation ultimately produces individuals who are responsible to participation' (1968, p. 109).

It seems probable that an element of participation will be introduced into the work life of many individuals in the future under the influence of the new theories of management that have been developed in the last decade or so. Whereas the more orthodox management theory is derived from Taylor's scientific management doctrines, and from the writings of theorists like Urwick who emphasise the pyramid-shaped authority structure, the chain of command, the span of control and so on, the new theories have their origins in modern psychological theories such as that of Maslow, and the human relations movement that grew out of the famous Hawthorne experiments. It was the latter that gave rise to the

[1] Verba (1961), pp. 173–5; see also pp. 227–8.

argument that efficiency depended not so much on the mechanical or technical aspects of the job, or on the correct organisational structure, but rather on the 'human element' in industry. It was the Hawthorne experiments that demonstrated (or, at least, are widely held to have done so) the crucial importance of interpersonal relationships in the workplace and the approach (style) of the supervisor.[1] Modern writers such as Mc-Gregor or Likert are sometimes referred to as neo-human relationists, and, like their forerunners, they emphasise the importance of the right interpersonal 'climate' in the enterprise. McGregor's theory in *The Human Side of Enterprise* and Likert's in *New Patterns of Management* are built on the evidence of the superiority of the 'participatory' style of supervision. Likert (1961) provides an interesting example of how participation might be introduced into the management structure of an enterprise in the future. He argues that, for efficiency, the management structure should be built round work groups organised on a participatory basis (or according to the principle of 'supportive relationships'). These groups are linked into the overall organisation by means of individuals 'who hold overlapping group membership. The superior in one group is a subordinate in the next group, and so on through the organisation' (p. 105). This means that 'different levels in the organisation should not be thought of in terms of more or less authority but rather as co-ordinating or linking larger or smaller numbers of work groups'.[2] If this form of organisation is to be effective the flow of communication and information has to be downward and sideways as well as upward. 'The giving and sharing of information is an essential step in the process of participation' (p. 243).

Blumberg has said of the empirical material on participation in the workplace that 'there is hardly a study in the entire literature which fails to demonstrate that satisfaction in work is enhanced or that other

[1] The reports of the Hawthorne experiments have recently been subjected to a searching examination by Carey (1967), and he concludes, after some stringent criticisms of the way in which they were conducted, that 'the limitations of the Hawthorne studies clearly render them incapable of yielding serious support for any sort of generalisation whatever'. Blumberg devotes two chapters of his book to a reinterpretation of the Hawthorne studies, but in view of Carey's criticisms, of which he makes no mention, it seems as dubious to cite the Hawthorne material in support of a thesis about participation as in support of anything else.

[2] Likert (1961, p. 186). Likert emphasises that it is necessary for the supervisor in one group—who is a subordinate in the next—to be able to participate in decision making in that group also or otherwise he may not be able, because of his lack of influence, to meet aspirations and expectations in his own group, raised by the experience of a participatory environment. That is, where such circumstances do not obtain, a 'participatory' style of supervision could lead to *dissatisfaction* among employees (Likert, p. 113). See also Blumberg (1968, pp. 116–17).

generally acknowledged beneficial consequences accrue from a genuine increase in workers' decision making power. Such consistency of findings, I submit, is rare in social research' (1968, p. 123). This is quite true; it is very difficult indeed to find anything that suggests otherwise. Partly, this may be due to the fact that so many different effects are involved; participation does usually seem to act positively on job satisfaction, for instance, but an increase in the latter may not always go together with an increase in another factor, say worker co-operation with management, so that results may depend on the precise form of interest in any one case.[1] One objection is certainly not valid, it has been suggested that participation is effective only in unit or craft production settings. The evidence cited above from the car and mining industries shows that this view is mistaken. It has also been suggested that participation is of no use in crisis situations (see Blumberg, p. 132). Whether this is true or not is irrelevant for our purposes, for we are interested in participation in everyday, non-crisis situations, in participation in the workplace. Here all the evidence indicates that not only will participation have a favourable effect on the individual in relation to the development of the sense of political efficacy, but that also it will not harm the efficiency of the enterprise, indeed it may increase it.

The major arguments of the theory of participatory democracy on the politically important psychological impact of participation in non-governmental authority structures, and the central role of industry in the democratic socialisation process, have been shown to have considerable empirical support. Moreover it has been found that participation at the level of the immediate work process is desired by most workers. The evidence indicates that it would be feasible to introduce participation at this level and many recent theories of management argue that such a participatory system is the most efficient way to run an enterprise. But if all this is true of participation at shop floor level, nothing has yet been said about participation in decisions affecting the wider affairs of the enterprise, or on the question of the democratisation of the overall authority structure. Before the evidence on this aspect can be fruitfully examined or the issues involved can be clarified it is necessary to analyse the concept of participation as applied to the industrial context, and investigate the relationship between 'participation' and 'industrial democracy'.

[1] On this example see the remarks in Lupton (1963, p. 201).

CHAPTER IV

'Participation' and 'democracy' in industry

Although the notion of 'participation' is widely used by writers on management topics it is, in many cases, left undefined, or if a definition is offered, that definition is very imprecise. McGregor (1960, p. 124), for example, after remarking that 'participation is one of the most misunderstood ideas that have emerged from the field of human relations', goes on to say that participation

consists basically in creating opportunities under suitable conditions for people to influence decisions affecting them. That influence can vary from a little to a lot . . . [participation] is a special case of delegation in which the subordinate gains greater control, greater freedom of choice, with respect to his own responsibilities. The term participation is usually applied to the subordinate's greater influence over matters within the superior's responsibilities (pp. 126 and 130).

Another typical definition of 'participation' is:

participation is any or all of the processes by which employees other than managers contribute positively towards the reaching of managerial decisions which affect their work (Sawtell, 1968, p. 1).

A third definition states that participation in decision making is:

the totality of such forms of upward exertions of power by subordinates in organisations as are perceived to be legitimate by themselves and their superiors (Lammers, 1967, p. 205).

Likert is an example of a writer who does not offer a definition of participation, but he and McGregor put forward a continuum of situations to which the term 'participation' can be applied; or rather, a continuum which ranges from a situation of 'a little' participation to 'a lot'. 'A little' participation in McGregor's continuum is a situation where subordinates can question a manager about his decision, and at the opposite end one where the superior is indifferent to several alternatives so that employees can choose between them (1960, pp. 126–7). The continuum presented by Likert (1961) covers a rather wider range of possibilities; from a situation of 'little participation'—'no information given to employees, either about the current situation or in advance of proposed changes'—to the situation where 'subordinates and leader functioning as a group tackle the problem and solve it, using the best available methods for group functioning' (p. 243).

To include such a very wide range of authority situations under the general heading of 'participatory' is to obscure the issues involved; for the notion of participation to be at all useful in dealing with the problems involved in industrial democracy (or with general management problems) a much more rigorous analysis must be attempted. There is one definition available, however, which does enable a start to be made in this direction and some useful distinctions drawn. French, Israel and Aas (1960) say that 'participation' in the industrial sphere refers to 'a process in which two or more parties influence each other in making plans, policies or decisions. It is restricted to decisions that have future effects on all those making the decisions and on those represented by them.' This definition, they say, excludes the following situations: where an individual, A, merely takes part in a group activity; where A is merely given information on a decision affecting him before it is executed; where A is present at a meeting but has no influence (p. 3).

This definition makes clear that participation must be participation *in* something; in this case participation in decision making (cf. the definition in the participatory theory of democracy). Now in ordinary speech we do use the term 'participation' in a very wide sense to cover almost any situation where some minimal amount of interaction takes place, often implying little more than that a particular individual was present at a group activity. In the definition above this very wide sense is rightly excluded. The whole point about industrial participation is that it involves a modification, to a greater or lesser degree, of the orthodox authority structure; namely one where decision making is the 'prerogative' of management, in which workers play no part. This is what is overlooked by many writers on management. In the definitions and 'continua' given above many situations are included that would be excluded by the French, Israel, Aas definition. That writers on management do not discriminate more carefully between different 'participatory' situations is not surprising when one considers their reason for being interested in participation in the workplace. For them, it is jut one management technique among others that may aid the achievement of the overall goal of the enterprise—organisational efficiency. Participation may, as we have seen, be effective in increasing efficiency, but what is important is that these writers use the term 'participation' to refer not just to a method of decision making, but also to cover techniques used to persuade employees to accept decisions that have *already* been made by the management. Situations of this type, where no participation in decision making in fact takes place, we shall, following Verba, call *pseudo participation*. A typical example would be the situation where the supervisor, instead of merely telling the employees of a decision, allows them to question him about it and to discuss it. In fact, many of the so-called 'participation' experiments with small groups were of this form. As Verba points out, often the concern was not to set up a situation where participation (in decision making) took place, but to create a *feeling* of participation through the adoption by the leader (supervisor) of a certain approach or style; 'participation' was thus 'limited to member endorsements of decisions made by the leader who . . . is neither selected by the group nor responsible to the group for his actions . . . the group leader, has a particular goal in mind and uses the group discussion as a means of inducing acceptance of the goal.' Verba adds that it is, in particular, in the field of industrial psychology that 'participatory leadership has become a technique of persuasion rather than of decision'.[1]

Having distinguished situations of pseudo-participation, participation in decision making itself can now be examined more closely. Firstly, it should be noted that if such participation is to take place then there is a necessary condition that must be met. That is, that employees must be in possession of the requisite information on which they can base their decision (cf. the quotation from Likert on p. 65). This, of course, is obvious enough in theory, but in practice it would mean considerably more information being given to employees than is usually the case at present.

The definition that we have taken as a starting point cannot be accepted as it stands. It states that 'participation' is a process 'in which two or more parties influence each other in making . . . decisions'. In particular the use of the words 'influence' and 'parties' needs more examination. In the theory of participatory democracy 'political equality' refers to equality of political power in determining the outcome of decisions, and 'power', Laswell and Kaplan (1950, p. 75) have said, 'is participation in the making of decisions'. Although the terms 'influence' and 'power' are very closely related to each other they are not synonymous, and it is significant that, in the definitions quoted, the former is usually used. To be in a position to influence a decision is not the same thing as to be in a position to (to have the power to) determine the outcome or to make that decision. Following Partridge (1963), we can say that 'influence' is applicable to a situation where individual A affects individual B, without B subordinating his

---

[1] Verba (1961, pp. 220–1). One reason that Stephens (1961) gives for the introduction of job enlargement is to enable employees to *feel* as if they are participating cf. also Bell's comment on the human relations management school, 'the ends of the enterprise remain, but the methods have shifted and the older modes of overt coercion are now replaced by psychological persuasion' (Bell, 1960, p. 244).

wishes to those of A (p. 111). That is to say, A has influence over B, and over the making of a decision, but it is B that has the power finally to decide. The use of the word 'parties' in the definition ('two or more parties influence each other') implies an opposition between two sides, which is in fact the usual case in the industrial situation, the 'parties' in question being the management and men. Furthermore, the final power of decision rests with the management, the workers if they are able to participate, being able only to influence that decision. Because they are 'workers' they are in the (unequal) position of permanent subordinates; the final 'prerogative' of decision making rests with the permanent superiors, with management. This type of participatory situation we shall refer to as *partial participation*; partial because A, the worker, does not have equal power to decide the outcome of decisions but can only influence them. Thus the French, Israel, Aas definition can be amended to read that 'partial participation is a process in which two or more parties influence each other in the making of decisions but the final power to decide rests with one party only'.[1]

Most of the examples of participation in the workshop in the last chapter were of partial participation, and of participation at what can be called the lower level of management. This lower level refers broadly to those management decisions relating to control of day-to-day shop floor activity, while the higher level refers to decisions that relate to the running of the whole enterprise, decisions on investment, marketing and so forth. Partial participation is possible at either level of management. Two of the empirical examples of participation given previously, however, illustrate a second form of lower level participation. These were the examples of the collective contract in the mining and car industries. There groups of workers operated virtually unsupervised by the management as self-regulating groups that made their own decisions about the everyday work process. In this kind of situation (in this example only at the lower level) there are not two 'sides' having unequal decision making powers,

[1] In practice in any particular case it might be difficult to distinguish the situation where actual influence does occur from the pseudo-participation situation, where it does not. But the theoretical distinction is clear. An important point is that the partial participation or 'influence' situation, must be distinguished from another, where although 'influence' occurs, no participation at all takes place. This is the case where Friedrich's 'law of anticipated reactions' comes into play. An example in the industrial context would be where the management of an enterprise is drawing up a list of alternatives from which a final policy decision will be made, but a theoretically possible alternative—say a wage cut—is not included as a practical possibility because union strength makes it impossible. Here the union has influenced the final decision but no participation has taken place.

but a group of equal individuals who have to make their own decisions about how work is to be allocated and carried out. Situations of this type we shall call situations of *full participation*; that is, this form of participation is 'a process where each individual member of a decision-making body has equal power to determine the outcome of decisions'. Like partial participation, full participation is possible at either the lower or higher management level, or both.[1]

With the distinction between partial and full participation established, we can now turn to the question of the relationship between participation and democracy in industry. Just as the term 'participation' is used extremely loosely in much of the literature, so is the concept of 'democracy'. Not only are the two words frequently used interchangeably but often 'democracy' refers not to a particular type of authority structure but to the general 'climate' that exists in the enterprise; a climate that is created through the method of approach, or style, of the supervisor or manager, i.e. 'democracy' is often used to describe situations of pseudo-participation or even merely to indicate that a friendly atmosphere exists. As has been pointed out in a criticism of the use of the term 'democracy' in the original Lewin experiments, the assumption was that democracy would 'result naturally from a person-to-person feeling in tolerant and generous community living'.[2] It is also frequently claimed that industrial democracy *already* exists in most industrialised Western countries. Perhaps the best known expression of this view is that of H. A. Clegg, one of the foremost British

[1] This particular usage of the term 'participation' departs from that of many writers, who regard it as referring to a situation of shared or joint decision making, involving two sides, the only alternative being seen as unilateral decision making by one side or the other. (See e.g. Sawtell, 1968, pp. 3 and 28.) A similar view seems to be held by a present-day advocate of industrial democracy and workers' control as this (rather extreme) passage indicates. 'Participation has the closest and ugliest relationship with a whole train of mean and sleazy predecessors in the sequence of devices for "heading off" a growing working class demand for control' (Coates, 1968, p. 228). While this view reflects the fact that 'participation' has frequently been used to mean no more than pseudo-participation it does illustrate the lack of clarity in most discussions of industrial participation and democracy. It overlooks the fact that 'control' and 'participation' do not represent alternatives, rather there can be no control without participation, how much depending on the form of participation. There is no good reason for confining 'participation' to a situation where there are two sides, for, as will be shown below, where industrial democracy exists there are no longer 'sides' in the existing sense.

[2] Kariel (1956, p. 288). Significantly enough the original experiments were with ten-year-old boys. Essentially all the 'democratic' style of leadership did was to put the boys in the kind of 'child-centred' environment that they might find today in a modern school, staffed by teachers well versed in up-to-date teaching methods and educational psychology.

experts on industrial matters, in his book *A New Approach to Industrial Democracy* (1960). It is especially interesting from our point of view that Clegg bases his arguments on recent theoretical writing on political democracy, i.e. on the writing of the advocates of the contemporary theory of democracy. However, Clegg's statement that 'in all the stable democracies there is a system of industrial relations which can fairly be called the industrial parallel of political democracy '(p. 131), simply is not correct. He argues that recent democratic theory has shown that the main requirement for democracy is the existence of an opposition (p. 19). In industry this opposition is provided by the trade unions with the employers (the management) performing the role of 'government'. It is not the latter analogy which is objectionable; the point is that the whole comparison of the authority situation in industry with the contemporary theory of democracy is not a valid one. As several commentators have pointed out—here in the words of Ostergaard—in industry 'the government (the management) is permanently in office, is self-recruiting, and is not accountable to anyone, except formally to the shareholders (or the state)'.[1] It would be a most curious kind of 'democratic' theorist who would argue for a government permanently in office and completely irreplaceable! In the contemporary theory of democracy, of course, the defining characteristic is just that there are replaceable, competing teams of leaders.

If the authority structure in industry is to be a real parallel to that of the national political system then the 'government' must be elected by, and removable by, the whole body of employees in each enterprise, or alternatively, for a direct democratic system, the whole body of employees must take the management decisions. In either case whether the democratic system was representative or direct it would mean that the present distinction between the management, permanently in office, and the men, permanent subordinates, was abolished. Where the whole body of employees took the decisions, then the management would merely be the men in a different capacity. A system of industrial democracy implies the opportunity for full higher level participation by employees. On the other

---

[1] Ostergaard (1961, p. 44). Clegg also argues that industrial democracy can have no other meaning than the one he gives it because 'it is impossible for the workers to share directly in management' (p. 119). This is a most odd claim. We have already seen that workers *can* share (participate) in (lower level) management, and Clegg not only refers to the example of the collective contract without appearing to realise its significance, but does not see that through collective bargaining, on which he lays such stress, partial participation in management is also possible (see further below). For a more extended, recent criticism of Clegg's book see Blumberg (1968, ch. 7).

hand, partial higher level participation does not require the democratisation of authority structures, for it is possible for workers, or their representatives, to influence higher level decisions while the final decision-making prerogative remains in the hands of the (permanent) management, as it does under the present collective bargaining situation. How far it would be possible to have a direct democratic situation within the industrial context, and how many workers would take up opportunities for participation in a democratised system are questions that cannot be considered until the relevant empirical evidence has been examined.

This analysis makes clear that, in the industrial context, the terms 'participation' and 'democracy' cannot be used interchangeably: they are not synonyms. Not only is it possible for partial participation at both management levels to take place without a democratisation of authority structures, but it is also possible for full participation to be introduced at the lower level within the context of a non-democratic authority structure overall. This has significance for the participatory theory of democracy. In that theory the implication is that to obtain the required psychological effect from participation, for the sense of political competence or efficacy to be developed, democratisation, i.e. full participation at the higher level, is required. In the contemporary theory of democracy, on the other hand, it is suggested that 'social training' is possible inside existing industrial authority structures. A consideration of the relationship between the psychological effects that have been found to accrue from participation, and the different forms of participation shows that the participatory theory of democracy requires modification in this respect. Perhaps the most striking fact that emerges from the empirical evidence is that participation is apparently so effective in its psychological impact on individuals even in the smallest possible doses; it appears that even the mere feeling that participation is possible, even situations of pseudo-participation, have beneficial effects on confidence, job satisfaction, etc.[1] It would be reasonable to suppose that actual participation would be more effective—if only because pseudo-participation may well raise expectations that could only be frustrated; as Blumberg says (1968, p. 79) so far as the psychological effects are concerned, the empirical evidence shows that 'what is crucial . . . is the ability and power of a group to arrive at a decision'.

Lower level partial participation is certainly favourable for the develop-

---

[1] This might be expected when one considers that participatory techniques are now quite often used for therapeutic purposes in the mental health field. One of the more radical experiments on these lines is described in Sugarman (1968). Blumberg (1968) also mentions that self-government experiments have been tried in American prisons (pp. 135–8).

ment of feelings of political efficacy; in fact this was shown by the five-nation survey of political attitudes from which we quoted in Chapter III. There, Almond and Verba's criteria of participation were presented without comment; whether the respondents were consulted when decisions were made on the job, whether they felt free to protest about decisions and whether they actually protested. Obviously, this 'participation' is at most partial participation, yet a positive correlation was found between it and a high score on the political efficacy scale. Thus so far as the development of the feeling of political efficacy is concerned democratisation of industrial authority structures is not required; therefore the theory of participatory democracy requires revision in this respect.

It would be mistaken to conclude at this point that any greater revision is required. So far only one aspect of the participatory theory has been dealt with—the prerequisites for a democratic polity at national level—and that only from the point of view of the development of the sense of political efficacy. Two points can be made here; firstly, that we have no means of knowing how effective the different forms of participation are; it might be that for maximum psychological effect higher level participation is needed. Secondly, although the evidence indicates that a sense of political efficacy is necessary for a politically active citizenry, it is not clear that it is sufficient. Almond and Verba's evidence suggests that it is not, for fewer respondents had actually tried to influence local or national government than felt able to do so (Tables VI.I and VI.2). We might recall here that the development of the sense of political efficacy was only part of the meaning of the educative effect of participation. Mill and Rousseau emphasised the broadening of outlook and interests, the appreciation of the connection between private and public interests, that the experience of participation would bring, and there is also 'education' in a more direct sense, the gaining of familiarity with democratic procedures and the learning of political (democratic) skills. For education in this sense higher level participation would seem to be required, for only participation at this level could give the individual experience in the management of collective affairs in industry and insight into the relationship between decisions taken in the enterprise and their impact on the wider social and political environment.

There is also another reason for paying attention to higher level participation in industry. Eckstein has argued that because industrial authority structures cannot be democratised then, for stability, governmental authority structures must be congruent and contain a 'healthy dose of authoritarianism'. But even if, as he claims, industrial democracy is impossible, it might still be possible to modify industrial authority structures in a democratic direction through the introduction of partial higher level participation, and so lessen the need for non-democratic elements at national government level.

It is to some empirical examples of higher level partial participation within British industry that I shall now turn. There are three interesting, and fairly well documented examples which are often referred to as examples of industrial democracy. The question of the psychological impact of participation will now be set aside, and instead attention will be focused on another problem in the theory of participatory democracy: how these forms of organisation work in practice and the extent to which workers are interested in, and take up, the opportunities for participation offered. Our first example is that of the Glacier Metal Company which employs about 5,000 people.[1] The organisational form that participation takes at Glacier is an extension of the normal collective bargaining and joint consultation machinery of British industry. Partial participation has been institutionalised by formalising and extending, through representative bodies, these usual procedures, while leaving the orthodox, hierarchical management structure intact.[2] Employee participation is based on the 'clear distinction between managerial authority to make decisions and give instructions, and employee participation in formulating the policy framework within which managers are sanctioned and freed to make those decisions' (Jaques, 1968, p. 1). Under the written constitution of the Company, participation takes place through a system—the 'legislative' system —of elected Works Councils in each of the Company's units. Their com-

---

[1] They are employed in several geographically separated factories. For the theory behind the organisation see Jaques (1951) and (1968); Brown (1960). For an empirical study of the Kilmarnock factory see Kelly (1968).

[2] It was mentioned earlier that collective bargaining enables the workers to partially participate in some management decisions. It might be thought that this participation by the unions differs from that of individual workers in the participation experiments, but in both cases the ultimate power of decision is regarded as a management 'prerogative'; finally the management have the power of lock-out or complete closure of the enterprise. Cf. this comment of Russell, 'the power of the industrialist . . . rests, in the last analysis, upon the lock-out, that is to say, upon the fact that the owner of a factory can call upon the forces of the state to prevent unauthorised persons from entering it' (Russell, 1938, p. 124). The scope of the Glacier experiment is especially interesting because collective bargaining at present tends to cover only lower level matters, and attempts to extend it are usually resisted by management as an illegitimate encroachment on their 'prerogatives'. This notion of 'prerogatives' is usually derived from the ownership of private property (but for a defence of 'prerogatives' which derives the notion from the 'nature of man' see O'Donnell (1952)). Recently the whole idea of the existence of managerial 'prerogatives' has come under attack on theoretical grounds, and its alleged legal basis has also been disputed. See Chamberlain (1958, ch. 12), and (1963); Young (1963); Chandler (1964).

position is based on the principle of 'each main layer in the factory's organisational hierarchy having representation on the Council' (Jaques, 1951, p. 139). Each Council consists of the Chief Executive of the area, one representative of senior, two of middle level staff, three of clerical and other staff, and the rank and file worker is represented by seven shop stewards. The Councils meet monthly and any member can request that a subject be placed on the agenda (any employee can attend the meetings as a spectator). The Councils are policy-making bodies and their main task is the working out of written policy documents and 'standing orders'; under the constitution management and men have agreed that no policy change shall be made unless all agree to it unanimously (Jaques, 1968, p. 2)

In theory, the scope of the Councils is clearly extremely wide. Subjects discussed have included wage systems, redundancy, factory closure and night shifts, but in practice (as this list might indicate) the highest level policy decisions do not come in the purview of the Council. At Glacier, 'top-policy making is the prerogative of the Board of Directors and Management. The directors authorise capital expenditure, decide dividends, appoint the Managing Director, decide director's fees, confirm senior appointments ... To say nothing of deciding who will "take over" the Company and so on'.[1] In addition to the introduction of elected participatory bodies, the other side of the Glacier experiment is an attempt to clarify and systematise the formal role definitions and relationships of management and men. The pre-1950 emphasis on group participation in decision making has shifted, in Kelly's review, to this other aspect.[2] There would seem to be something inherently contradictory in this attempt *both* to operate a system where employees can participate in all policy decisions, and one that sharpens and systematises (and enshrines in a company language) the difference in authority between 'managers' and 'subordinates'.

At the Kilmarnock factory (the only one on which empirical material is available) the Council has been regarded with considerable suspicion; after a strike in 1957 it was renamed the 'Works Committee' and the Company policy document has only recently been accepted by the shop stewards.[3] This may account for the fact that at Council meetings the

---

[1] Kelly (1968, p. 248); see also Jaques (1968, p. 2).

[2] Kelly (1968, p. 26). This involves an internal 'role language' and the use of command meetings, which, as their name implies, are largely concerned with the issuing of managerial orders (and also the assessment of employees). 'It would appear, going on impressions, that the word most frequently used in the Company is "subordinate"' (Kelly, p. 278. See also pp. 251 and 232).

[3] Kelly (1968, p. 241). The cultural background of the factory differs considerably to the London one, but no information is available on the latter. See pp. 97–100.

representatives of the rank and file show little interest in matters such as the annual report and accounts or even investment decisions; at least, little discussion takes place on these topics unless individual departments are affected, and most discussion occurs on lower levels matters. At the meeting attended by Kelly the Chairman and General Manager spoke for 74% of the time (pp. 242–5). This organisational form of higher level partial participation is obviously particularly suited to British industrial conditions and it would, potentially, allow employees to participate in the full range of decision making. At Glacier though, from the point of view of the management, one of its major effects has been to legitimise the decision-making powers constitutionally retained by them. In the light of the discussion of the effects of lower level participation in the last chapter, this comment by Jaques is one that might be expected, 'the experience of managers at Glacier Metal has on the whole showed that this constitution enables them to make far more decisions and changes without objections from representatives than is customary in other companies' (Jaques, 1968, p. 4).

The largest experiment in higher level partial participation in Britain is that of the John Lewis Partnership (which includes the department stores), and an excellent study of this has been published, from which this information is taken.[1] Although the orthodox authority structure has been modified further than at Glacier, in practice in the Partnership, the representative bodies act rather as efficient consultative mechanisms than as decision-making bodies.

As described in the house journal, 'the supreme purpose of the whole organisation is to secure the fairest possible sharing by all members of all the advantages of ownership—gain, knowledge and power'.[2] The first two of these aims are met at present to a greater degree than the third. All shares in the Partnership are held by a Trust and all distributed profits are shared by the partners (employees). All partners are equal in the sense that all share the rewards so that, in this formal sense, the Partnership has gone some way to meeting the condition of economic equality regarded as necessary for participation by the theorists of participatory democracy. However, distribution is according to level of pay, so that in a practical sense there is no move to economic equality; this distribution 'accentuates the prevailing hierarchical structure of remuneration'.[3] We have seen

---

[1] Flanders, Pomeranz and Woodward (1968). This includes a brief history of the Partnership.

[2] Quoted Flanders et al. (1968, p. 42).

[3] Flanders et al., p. 185. For workers' attitudes to the profit-sharing scheme, some of whom favour a redistributive scheme, see pp. 102–6.

that the possession of the requisite information is a necessary condition for participation, and in the Partnership the 'sharing of knowledge' is furthered through the internal press (to which anonymous letters are encouraged, and answered) and a general meeting open to all partners, held yearly in each branch. The Central and Branch Councils also have annual trading accounts made available to them.[1]

The Councils are the major means through which participation can take place, but the rank and file partner is under-represented on them and the scope of his participation remains potential rather than actual. The Central Council has rights which do give it certain sanctions against the Chairman and Board, if the need arose; it appoints three Trustees of the Constitution, who then become directors, and it also nominates five other directors. The main day-to-day function of the Central Council is the administration of a large welfare fund, but it is entitled to 'discuss any matter whatsoever and make any suggestion that they shall see fit to the Central Board or to the Chairman'.[2] However, the Council does not normally conduct detailed policy discussions, so that although, theoretically, it has very wide scope its actual participatory influence would appear to be very limited (p. 177). The Central Council has 140 members, about three-quarters elected and the rest appointed by the Chairman of the Partnership including all senior management. Candidates for the Council elections come from all ranks of partners, but those standing and elected are more likely to be of managerial status than the rank and file. From 1957–8 to 1966–7 the proportion of managerial rank councillors has varied from 61% to 70% (plus 20% to 24% ex officio members) and that of rank and file partners from 8% to 19%.[3] In the sub-committees, which carry out a large part of the work, there is a marked shift to higher management membership.

The Branch Councils, modelled on the Central Council and subordinate to it, are somewhat more representative of the rank and file, who comprise about half the elected membership. (The councils average 35 members, about 15% ex officio.) Apart from administering its own welfare funds the Branch Council can sponsor resolutions to the Central Council, which, if adopted, become recommendations to management. About six to

---

[1] Flanders et al., pp. 76 and 42 ff. Secrecy is maintained over wages, a source of grievance to many partners. Committees for Communication exist, which are solely rank and file bodies. These are essentially grievance-settling bodies that have no funds or executive powers and cannot themselves take remedial action, so are of little relevance from the participatory point of view (see p. 50 ff.).

[2] Flanders et al. (1968, p. 64). For nomination powers, etc., see pp. 64–5.

[3] Flanders et al., p. 60, Table 5. Twenty-two per cent of men and 25% of women candidates had held some special status in the Partnership (p. 84).

seven a year are made and from 1955 to 1964 a third were accepted, though not all implemented.[1] It was a Branch Council that, for the first time, rejected a major management proposal (on five-day trading). During the previous discussions on this issue, in the opinion of the authors of the study, 'the decision process itself was basically the normal one of management deciding what it wanted to achieve, and preparing the ground in such a way that orders issued were likely to be obeyed'.[2] The policy rejection was accepted by the Chairman of the Partnership—though it should be noted that no vital trading issues were involved—but whether this incident indicates that in future partners will make more use of their participatory powers remains to be seen.

The level of interest in, and knowledge of, the representative institutions, is low.[3] The authors of the study found that, among full-time rank and file partners, those most interested were men and women of over five years' service, but even in this group interest declined in the higher level bodies.[4] The structure of the representative bodies of the Partnership may itself be partly responsible for the lack of interest. In fact, many partners did display an interest in lower level participation, which confirms the evidence on this point cited earlier, but the scope of the participatory institutions does not cover many lower level matters, and the general finding was that about two-thirds of the respondents 'did not show any marked degree of interest in the Partnership's democratic institutions' (p. 127).

Our third example is the Scott Bader Commonwealth, a plastic resin manufacturing company in Wollaston, Northants, employing about 350 persons.[5] This company has made much more far reaching changes in the orthodox industrial authority structure than our two other examples of

[1] P. 72. These resolutions include such matters as alterations in the rules for life assurance and pensions. Few proposals in the Central Council come from either the Branch Councils or individual councillors. See p. 68, Table II.

[2] Flanders et al., p. 176. As the authors point out, it is difficult for middle management Council members to oppose official policy (p. 174).

[3] How far this helps explain the relative lack of use of participation opportunities, or how far the fact that the representative bodies often seem to act as pseudo-participatory devices explains the lack of interest, it is impossible to say. It is very significant, however, that about two-thirds of the employees are women because all empirical investigations of social and political participation have shown that women tend to participate less than men. See Milbrath (1965, pp. 135–6).

[4] Flanders et al., pp. 86 and 114–16, Tables 25, 26. A high proportion of women answered 'don't know' to a question on whether they would be sorry to see the institutions given up.

[5] This company, too, has been the subject of a recently published study, Blum (1968). Additional information can be found in Hadley (1965); also see Exley (1968) and publications of Scott Bader & Company Limited.

higher level partial participation. The firm was deliberately re-organised along participatory lines in 1951 by its founder, Ernest Bader, and opportunities for participation were increased in 1963 when the institutions were further modified. All the shares of Scott Bader & Company Limited are held communally by a charitable organisation, the Scott Bader Commonwealth Limited (in the event of the company's sale the proceeds are to go to charity). Membership of the Commonwealth is open to all employees after a probationary period.[1]

The organisational structure of the Commonwealth is a rather complex one. The main 'legislative' body is the General Meeting, which meets quarterly, and where each member of the Commonwealth has one vote. Its powers cover the approval, modification or rejection of the conduct of the business, the right of approval of any investment over £10,000 before it is made, and approval of the disposal of the common surplus (profits) recommended by the Community Council and Board of Directors.[2] The Community Council of the Commonwealth is the main 'administrative' body, composed of twelve persons; nine are elected, two nominated by the Board, and one, representing the local community, is nominated by Council and approved by the Board. Apart from its function relating to the common surplus, the Council is concerned with welfare facilities and with the rules of membership of the Commonwealth, individual applications being decided on merit. A novel feature of the organisation is the Panel of Representatives. This is a body of twelve members who are chosen at random from all Commonwealth members and they have to decide whether 'the conditions and atmosphere that exists in the firm justify them in recording a vote of confidence in the Board of Directors'.[3]

Before looking at what actually happens inside this organisational

---

[1] In 1961 there were 143 members from a total of 266 employees. Blum (1968, p. 98). Blum says that most non-members were not yet eligible, having not then served the two-year probationary period (now one year).

[2] A diagram of the structure can be found in Blum (1968, p. 157). Since 1965 the Community Council has recommended the method of distributing the 'bonus' part of the surplus, the Board of Directors determining its amount. The constitution provides that the surplus must be distributed within the ratio 60% plough-back, 20% charitable purposes and 20% employee 'bonus'. Recently the bonus has run between 5–10% (Blum, pp. 153 and 212).

[3] Blum (1968, p. 154). If the answer is 'no' a complicated procedure follows, but the final decision on what action, if any, is necessary devolves on the Trustees, whose main function is that of 'guardians' of the Constitution of the Commonwealth. Two of the Trustees are elected; see Blum, pp. 155 ff. and 164–5. There is another partially elected body, the Council of Reference, the final appeal body, mainly concerned with disciplinary questions.

structure, it is worth noting that the Scott Bader Commonwealth provides an interesting example of how an approach might be made toward economic equality in a modern society. In the Commonwealth the difference in status between employees has been considerably reduced. Firstly, all Commonwealth members are equal in that all have one vote at the General Meeting. Secondly, all employees enjoy a high degree of job security, gross misconduct and incompetence being virtually the sole grounds for dismissal (and in all cases the appeal system operates). Thirdly, all employees are salaried and have a guaranteed minimum wage; there is also a limit on top salaries, the Constitution laying down that the ratio between the highest and lowest salary must not exceed 7:1. Members of the Commonwealth also have access to much more information about the affairs of the enterprise than those who work within more orthodox authority structures. Management must answer all questions raised in the internal newspaper, questions can be asked at the General Meeting, and there is a further provision that members have the right to inspect accounts and ask for information through representatives or in personal interviews with management.[1]

There are several channels through which participation can take place at Scott Bader, but the Constitution is hedged about by 'checks and balances', and up till now participation seems to be rather limited in practice. Unfortunately, in the only full length study available, Blum (1968) says very little about the Commonwealth's day-to-day practice.[2] However, it is clear that, as at the John Lewis partnership, levels of interest and participation among the employees with rank and file jobs are low. Blum says that 'there have been considerable differences in the participation of different groups ... Workers have undoubtedly participated less than other groups' (p. 329). In general, the proportion of total employees who have participated by holding office as a representative is fairly small because, from 1951 to 1963, thirty-four people served on the Community Council and 'a large majority' were re-elected for more than one term; about ten of those elected were from the shop floor.[3] It was found, using as criteria

[1] Blum (1968, pp. 84-5) and Hadley (1965). Clocking in has also been abolished. None of these fairly radical measures, or the participatory structure appears to have adversely affected economic performance; since 1951 annual turnover has increased ten times to £4m.

[2] An empirical investigation was carried out, but Blum refers to this material only in passing. His book is mainly concerned with an interpretation of the principles underlying the organisational forms, but this account, couched to a large extent in religio-metaphysical terminology, is far from clear.

[3] Blum, p. 96. The period of office is three years, which, in itself, limits the numbers who can participate.

of participation speaking at General Meetings, obtaining information from representatives, standing for election and initiating proposals through a participative body, that about a fifth of managers, technicians, junior managers and clerical workers were 'high' or 'moderate' participants, whereas *all* the factory workers were 'low' or non-participants (p. 374). For most of those questioned by Blum the 'advantages of the Commonwealth' were seen, particularly by the factory workers, first and foremost in terms of the job security it gave (including the six months' sick leave), although 'participation' was the item mentioned the next most frequently. Finally, in a question on the knowledge of the powers of the Community Council it was found that 26% of respondents had a 'working knowledge', 36% had a 'partial knowledge' and 38% 'little or no knowledge' (p. 375, also p. 99).

On the face of it the evidence from these three examples would seem to suggest that it is over-optimistic to expect the ordinary worker to avail himself of opportunities for higher level partial participation and that the conclusion should be that the contemporary theory of democracy is right to start with the fact of apathy as a basic datum. However, the evidence is capable of being interpreted in a different way. At Scott Bader, like the John Lewis Partnership, there are few opportunities for lower level participation and yet all our evidence has shown that ordinary workers are interested in this level.[1] It could be argued that lack of such opportunities where interest exists could lead to the higher level participation opportunities seeming remote from the rank and file worker, for little in his everyday work experience prepares him for these. It is significant that attitudes of employees at different job levels in the Commonwealth differ greatly as is illustrated by the question of the Board of Directors and the Founder Members' shares. Before 1963 the Founder Members had certain rights and held 10% of the shares and in 1957 Ernest Bader offered to transfer these shares to the Commonwealth. Discussion groups were formed to consider this proposal, reporting that it was acceptable providing that the right of electing directors was also vested in the Commonwealth. This Ernest Bader rejected. In 1959, Blum asked questions on both these points, and it was the managerial and laboratory workers who were mostly in favour, and the factory workers who were mostly against or uncertain about handing over the shares or electing the directors. 'What on earth would we do, we don't know who should

[1] Under the Commonwealth Constitution provision was made for Departmental Committees and these were set up in 1951 but never functioned regularly. Interest has recently revived in these so perhaps in the future participation opportunities may become available at the lower level. (See Hadley, 1965.)

go on the Board, only the higher ups know that', and 'No, the Founder shares shouldn't go to the Commonwealth, after all he founded the firm, it was his money in the first place' were typical comments from the latter (pp. 146–52). The difference in attitudes on this point might offer support for Cole's view of the 'training for subservience' received by most ordinary workers. That is to say, even in a situation where higher level opportunities are opened up for the ordinary worker, who has been socialised into the existing system of industrial authority structures and who still has no opportunity to participate every day at the lower level, notions such as the election of directors are frequently just not 'available', in the way that they are to higher status workers.[1]

We can now briefly summarise the results so far for the participatory theory of democracy, in its educative or socialisation aspect, of our examination of the empirical evidence on participation in industry. The only revision necessary is on the question of the development of the sense of political efficacy; lower level participation may well be sufficient for this. Turning to the wider educative effects of participation there seem to be few practical barriers to the institution of a system of higher level partial participation; certainly it appears compatible with economic efficiency. Thus, Eckstein's 'congruency' argument about the need for 'authoritarian' elements in national government requires modification in at least this respect. Unfortunately, owing to the isolated nature and the unique features of these three examples of higher level partial participation, it is difficult to draw firm general conclusions. In particular, we cannot hope to answer the important question of how far rank and file workers are likely to be interested in and to take up such participation opportunities until we have information on the effect of a system that combines both lower and higher level participation.

It is now possible to turn to the second aspect of the theory of participatory democracy; the argument that industry and other spheres form political systems in their own right and that they should therefore be democratised. Again, industry occupies a crucial position in the question of whether a participatory society is possible; industry, with its relationships of superiority and subordination, is the most 'political' of all areas in which ordinary individuals interact and the decisions taken there have a

[1] The element of paternalism present in the Commonwealth situation also has to be borne in mind when attitudes, etc., are considered. In the event, in 1963, the shares were handed over and the Founder Members' rights abolished but, as before, only two of the nine directors are to be elected by the Commonwealth (the list of candidates being approved by the Board). Five others are nominated by the Chairman and approved by the Trustees and the two Baders became life Directors.

great effect on the rest of their lives. Furthermore, industry is important because the size of the enterprise might allow the individual to participate directly in decision making, to participate fully at the higher level.[1] If the evidence shows, as has been claimed, that it it impossible to democratise industrial authority structures, then the theory of participatory democracy will require substantial revision.

[1] Cf. this argument of Bachrach's, 'If private organisations, at least the more powerful among them, were considered political—on the ground that they are organs which regularly share in authoritatively allocating values for society—then there would be a compelling case, in terms of the democratic principle of equality of power, to expand participation in decision-making within these organisations' (1967, p. 96).

CHAPTER V

Workers' self-management in Yugoslavia

It has been shown that a widespread demand for participation at lower management levels does exist among ordinary workers but this does not seem to be the case where higher level decisions are concerned, as the empirical material cited in the last chapter has illustrated. In the Norwegian survey referred to in Chapter III, Holter found that only 16% of blue collar and 11% of white collar workers wished they had more participation in decisions concerning the management of the whole firm.[1] In the recent study of the Vauxhall car workers a precisely comparable question was not asked, but the workers were asked whether they thought that unions should be solely concerned with pay and conditions or whether they should 'try and get workers a say in management'. Forty per cent of those questioned thought they should (61% of craftsmen) but the majority attitude can be illustrated by remarks like; 'the average person in a place like this likes to think he could manage, but management is really for educated people who can do it'.[2] The fact that a majority of the craftsmen wanted this wider role for the unions, and that those in Holter's survey who desired higher level participation were 'responsible, confident, skilled' is significant, given the facts about the development of the sense of political efficacy, and it adds further force to the suggestion made in the last chapter that for many of the lower level workers such ideas are simply not 'available'. As Holter puts it 'the atmosphere of hierarchical systems in general, the limited perspective inherent in the work of an operator or sub-clerical worker, may tend to lower beyond reasonable proportions the number of employees who are able to see themselves as participants in managerial tasks' (1965, p. 305). Thus little can be directly inferred from the overt lack of demand on the part of workers for participation at this level about the practical possibilities for industrial democracy.

Before any more empirical material is considered some clarification is necessary; clarification on exactly why it is claimed that it is impossible to democratise industrial authority structures, and this is a more difficult task

[1] Holter (1965, p. 301, Table 2, also p. 304, Table 3b).
[2] Goldthorpe *et al.* (1968, pp. 108–9, Table 47).

85

than one might expect. Eckstein (1966) is not very explicit; 'Some social relations simply cannot be conducted in a democratic manner, or can be so conducted only with the gravest dysfunctional consequences ... We have every reason to think that economic organisations cannot be organised in a truly democratic manner, at any rate not without consequences that no one wants' (p. 237). He goes on to say that the most we can hope for is some 'pretence' or 'simulation' of democracy but the only—quite extraordinary—example he gives of this is that certain economic organisations are willing to incur functional disadvantages and 'play a great deal at democracy' and do so by permitting 'certain deviations from the logic of the double-entry ledger in order actually to carry on certain democratic practices'. Apart from this odd statement he offers no evidence to support the argument that it is impossible and gives no indication of what the dysfunctional consequences are.[1] Presumably, what Eckstein has in mind are economic consequences, i.e. that a democratised system would not be capable of operating efficiently, or might even collapse. On the other hand, quite different interpretations might be given to the term 'impossible'. It might be argued (cf. the evidence cited above) that not enough workers would be interested, or would participate, to make the system viable; or (qua Michels) that real democratisation is not possible because, in practice, an elected, inexpert, part-time body could not really control the full-time expert staff who would really run things. But it is unlikely that Eckstein has such possibilities in mind; he merely asserts his case, he does not argue it. This assertion about the impossibility of democratising authority structures is another aspect of the normative nature of the contemporary theory of democracy. Since we already have the sort of democratic political system that we should have, we therefore have the right sort of 'prerequisites' also, in the form of existing non-governmental authority structures; any attempt to democratise these could only endanger the stability of the system. Nevertheless, we shall take the assertion seriously and look at some plausible interpretations of the alleged 'impossibility' in the course of the following discussion.

There is, in Britain and the U.S.A., a singular lack of examples of enterprises organised on democratic lines (or, rather, if they do exist they

[1] Eckstein (1966, p. 238). He also says that 'even certain kinds of public ownership (like nationalisation in Britain of industries absolutely vital to the health of the whole economy) militate against a democratisation of economic relations' (p. 237). But the whole point of the case of British nationalisation is that it provides no evidence at all; democratisation has bever been tried. This was the result of deliberate decision by the Labour Party (the 1945–51 Government) to adopt the 'Morrisonian formula' and to try nothing else. Thus a valuable opportunity to experiment was lost, and at a time when public opinion, and the workers, were in favour of real change.

are rarely written about). In Britain there is one example which almost exactly corresponds to our model of (direct) full participation at the higher level. Unfortunately, the Rowen Engineering Co. Limited, in Glasgow, is very small, approximately 20 employees, and the workers have tended to be self-selected, but it is of considerable intrinsic interest and useful for illustrative purposes.[1] The controlling body of the factory is the General Council, membership of which is open to all employees after three months' service, and each member has one vote. Meetings of the Council are held fortnightly, the agenda being displayed two days beforehand and any employee is entitled to add items to it. (Tea-break meetings are also held if the need arises but decisions must be ratified at the next Council meeting.) Each member occupies the chair for two meetings, which means that everyone has to participate verbally on at least these occasions (Derrick and Phipps, p. 105). The General Council decides on all policy matters and anything else of importance; it also elects the directors, the factory manager, the foreman and 'co-ordinator' (chargehand). At each meeting the Council receives reports on production, sales, finance, etc.[2] There is also a labour sub-committee to deal with personnel matters, but this does not make decisions, only recommendations to the Council.

A meeting of the General Council attended by Jarvie (1968, p. 20) illustrates how one of the problems mentioned above in connection with the 'impossibility' thesis can arise in the smallest organisation. At this meeting a member of the assembly department suggested that production should be stopped on a particular model of heater as some were being returned. The professionally trained sales engineer denied that the design was at fault and presented a technical report to substantiate this. This report was vigorously challenged and it was finally agreed to insti-

---

[1] Since one example exists, it clearly *is* possible to democratise industrial authority structures but no conclusions can be drawn from this example about the possibility of democratisation on the scale of a whole economy, which is what the idea of a participatory society demands. The factory was started in 1963 as a worker controlled 'factory for peace'. It received publicity in the peace movement and on the 'left', hence the element of self-selection. The name is derived from R(obert) Owen. (A second, similar, factory has been set up in Wales.) It is quite successful economically, starting with (mostly donated) capital of £7,000 and it now has a turnover in the region of £80,000 p.a. See Blum (1968, pp. 49–51); Derrick and Phipps (1969, pp. 104–7); Rowen Factories (1967) and Sawtell (1968, pp. 41–2), Companies A and B).

[2] Directors are required by law; however, their only duty at Rowen Engineering is to sign cheques (Jarvie, p. 15). There is also an Advisory Council, composed of representatives of organisations sympathetic to the aims of the factory, whose function is to ensure that General Council decisions do not infringe the principles on which the factory is based.

tute an inquiry into the design at issue. One might question whether, in a factory with a more representative labour force, such an 'expert' report would receive that kind of searching examination. This problem of the control of 'experts' by the ordinary (manager) worker will be discussed more fully below in connection with the industrial system in Yugoslavia. Yugoslavia, because that country provides, in the form of their workers' self-management system, the only available example of an attempt to introduce industrial democracy on a large scale, covering enterprises of many sizes and types over a whole economy.

No discussion of industrial participation and democracy can afford to ignore the Yugoslav system. It is also of considerable interest because, seen as a whole, the Yugoslav socio-political and industrial forms of organisation look, in many respects (at least formally), remarkably like Cole's blueprint for a participatory society. Here, however, we shall confine our attention to the industrial side to see what light the workers' management system might throw on the possibilities of democratising industrial authority structures. There are considerable difficulties involved in any such assessment; firstly, there is the problem of the availability of the necessary evidence. Although the number of English language studies of, and commentaries on, the Yugoslav industrial organisation are increasing, they are by no means as sufficient either in quantity or comprehensiveness, as one would wish. Secondly, there are the difficulties inherent in the Yugoslav situation itself. Yugoslavia is a relatively undeveloped country, with wide differences in development between the Republics.[1] Many factory workers still work part time on the land (the bulk of which is privately owned) and much of the labour force is composed of ill-educated, first generation, industrial workers.[2] Even in 1953, the average level of

[1] National Income 1964

	Billions of new dinars	£ per head	Population (millions)
Bosnia and Hercegovinia	6.8	56	3.5
Croatia	14.6	97	4.3
Macedonia	3.0	57	1.5
Montenegro	0.9	51	0.5
Serbia	21.5	78	7.9
Slovenia	9.0	161	1.6
Yugoslavia	55.8	83	19.3

From *The Economist*, 16 July 1966.

[2] In 25 years the rural population has been reduced from 75% to 45% of the whole (*The Economist*, 16 July 1966). One per cent to 2% of the increase in the industrial work force each year comes direct from the land (Auty, 1965, p. 159).

illiteracy in the population over ten years old, was 25.4% (for women 35.8%), so that allowance has to be made for these facts when the working of the workers' self-management system is assessed.[1] Yugoslavia is, of course, a Communist state, even though a rather different one from other Eastern European countries, so that the role of the Communist Party also has to be taken into account. Finally, the system of workers' self-management is, itself, of relatively recent origin. Introduced in 1950, after the break with the U.S.S.R. in 1948, it did not really get under way until new regulations and economic reforms were introduced in 1953, and, since then, the organisational forms and legal framework have undergone an almost continuous process of modification and change which adds to the difficulties of evaluation.

Firstly, let us consider the organisational structure of industry in Yugoslavia. Each industrial enterprise in Yugoslavia is managed by an elected Workers' Council, elected by the whole collective (i.e. all the employees) through electoral units in the larger enterprises. By law, all enterprises of more than seven workers must have a Council, but where there are less than thirty then all workers form the Council. In larger enterprises the size of the Workers' Council can range from 15 to 120 members, the average being from 20 to 22.[2] Large enterprises can also, if they wish, elect departmental Councils and, since 1961, a system of what the Yugoslavs call 'economic units' has been instituted. Each enterprise is divided into viable production units that can exercise a degree of self-management at that level. The organisation of these units is left to the individual enterprise. One study says that the management of the unit is 'in the hands of an Assembly of the whole membership' but at Rade Koncar (the biggest producer of electrical equipment in Yugoslavia) the units have their own Workers' Councils.[3] Apart from the Workers' Councils and the economic units, workers can also participate in decision making through meetings of the whole collective of the enterprise and by means of referenda on important topics.

Membership of the Council is for two years (members are subject to recall by their electorate) and the Council meets monthly. Workers' Councils have subcommittees to deal with certain matters; since 1957 they have been obliged to have them for internal discipline and hiring and firing. Membership of these committees is not necessarily restricted to

[1] I.L.O. (1962, App. 1, Table A).
[2] Blumberg (1968, p. 198). Private employers are limited to five employees outside the family.
[3] Singleton and Topham (1963, p. 15). For a description of the organisation of Rade Koncar see Kmetic (1967).

Council members.[1] The Workers' Council elects its executive body, the Managing Board, usually, but not necessarily entirely, from its own members. The Board has from 3 to 17 members (the Director ex officio) elected for one-year periods; if a member is elected twice in succession he is then ineligible for a further two years.[2] The Board may meet several times in a week and it has important functions including the supervision of the Director's work, ensuring the fulfilment of the plans of the enterprise, and the drawing up of the annual plan. The other legally obligatory 'organ of management', apart from the Council and its Board, is the Director of the enterprise. Since 1964 the final choice of applicant for the post (which is advertised) is in the hands of the Workers' Council, and the Director's term of office has been limited to four years.[3] The Director, together with the 'Collegium' of heads of departments, is responsible for the administration, the day-to-day running of the enterprise and execution of the Workers' Council decisions. He also has other powers legally defined, such as the power to sign contracts in the name of the enterprise, to represent it in dealings with external bodies and to ensure that the enterprise operates within the law.

Before seeing how all this works, it will be useful to look briefly at the economic performance of Yugoslavia under the workers' self-management system in order to ascertain if there are economic 'dysfunctions' so great as to render the system 'impossible' (though short of complete economic collapse that could be unambiguously attributed to the system, there are many difficulties over what would count as confirmatory evidence). By 1964 real income per head in Yugoslavia was almost four times greater than the pre-war level; over the decade to 1967 total output increased by an average of 8% p.a. and, since the war, the growth rate 'has been hardly less fast than Japan's'.[4] This is a creditable record, but not a straightforward success story. The sweeping economic reforms of 1965 were caused partly by inflationary and balance of payments problems; another factor was the desire to modernise techniques and to get rid of uneconomic investment. One writer quotes over-investment in the early 1960s as 'testimony to the

[1] Stephen (1967, p. 8), also Singleton and Topham (1963, p. 14) and Kmetic (1967, p. 13).
[2] Stephen (1967, p. 12). Regulations cited in Blumberg (1968, p. 205) are slightly different.
[3] Until 1952 he was appointed by the State and then by a Commission composed equally of representatives of the Workers' Council and the Commune. The Director can be removed by the Council but the procedure is not entirely clear. See Blumberg (1968, p. 205).
[4] *The Economist* 16 July 1966 and 19 August 1967.

autonomy of workers' management'[1] but, as their popular name implies, the so-called 'political factories' were a result of political rather than Workers' Council calculation. One problem is how far the Workers' Council system will act as an obstacle to modernisation, to the introduction of labour-saving techniques, etc. There is some evidence that Councils are reluctant to vote for redundancies, but under the orthodox Western management system successful modernisation depends a lot on general economic conditions, the level of employment and factors like the availability of redundancy payments, housing, retraining schemes and so on, and the same thing surely applies in Yugoslavia. It is impossible to say at this stage whether the Workers' Council system will pose insuperable difficulties (it may even be that Councils would take matters like social cost more readily into account than an orthodox management), but it does seem fairly clear that even if the economic expansion cannot be said to be a direct result of the system, at least it has not, up to the present, acted as a particular hindrance to economic expansion and efficiency. To test the thesis of the 'impossibility' of democratising industrial authority structures along Yugoslav lines we must, therefore, examine the internal working of the system. The first question that must be asked here is whether, given that Yugoslavia is a Communist state, the Workers' Councils do have any independent power at all (of course, even if they did not, nothing would follow from this about the possibilities of such a system in a different socio-political context).

There are several channels through which the Communist League (Party) can exercise influence or control over the Workers' Councils, but the role of the League itself is a profoundly ambiguous one. On the one side the League, in theory, no longer exercises control by direct rule, but it maintains its leading role through 'the strength of ideas and arguments', and there is continuing debate inside Yugoslavia about its role and the question of the separation of party and state. In practice, however, all 'the more important decisions about the development of the society are still taken centrally by a small group of party leaders'.[2] On the other hand—which illustrates the Jekyll and Hyde character of the League—it operates within a formally extremely participatory system and within an ideological view of a socialist society as 'one characterised by the conscious and or-

[1] Blumberg (1968, p. 213). For the economic reforms see Neal and Fisk (1966) and *The Economist*, 16 July 1966.

[2] Riddell (1968, p. 55). On developments in the position of the League after the fall of Rancovik in 1966 see Neal and Fisk (1966) and Rubinstein (1968). See also 'Draft Thesis on the Further Development and Reorganisation of the League of Communists of Yugoslavia' (1967).

ganised control by the members of society themselves of all the institutions of their society'.[1]

One channel through which the League can influence the Workers' Councils is by having its members elected to the Commune Assembly. The Commune (roughly analogous to British local government units) is the basic political unit in Yugoslavia, on which higher levels are built. Basically, chambers at all levels are divided into two, the 'municipal' chamber and the Chamber of Work Communities; 'the citizens figure in this socio-economic organisation both as individuals and as collectives in enterprises and institutions'.[2] (Other chambers also exist.) Nomination and election procedures to the Commune Assembly are very complicated (election is partly direct and partly indirect) but in recent years some element of choice does appear to have been introduced at elections.[3] The Communes have considerable local autonomy in government, and they are keenly interested in enterprises in their areas because a large part of their income depends upon the economic prosperity of the Commune. They have certain powers in relation to the individual enterprise, including the right to make recommendations about policy. Today, the enterprise seems to be a good deal more independent in this relationship than it did in the early days. As already noted, the control of the appointment of the Director is no longer shared with the Commune and, at least in the factories studied by one observer, the Workers' Council took an independent attitude with regard to proposals and requests from the Commune (Kolaja, 1965, pp. 28 and 62).

The League can also work through the Trade Unions, another organisation whose role, both generally and inside the enterprise, is ambiguous.[4]

[1] Riddell (1968, p. 55). This ideological position should not be dismissed out of hand as mere 'window dressing'. As Riddell points out, the history of Yugoslavia is one of a tradition of local autonomy and hostility to central authority and the Partisan movement was based largely on local groups and actions (today the League is organised on a Republic basis); also the Yugloslav leaders were familiar with anarcho-syndicalist as well as orthodox Marxist doctrines. In the industrial field, if the aim had been only to 'decentralise a socialised industry' (Rhenman, 1968, p. 6) or to give management more independence (the result of the system in one view; Kolaja, 1965, p. 75) or to provide a managerial class, then there would have been no need to set up these particular organisational forms; though this is not to say that all the consequences were either foreseen or intended. See also Deleon (1959) and Auty (1965) for a history of the establishment of the present system.

[2] Milivojevic (1965, p. 9). In 1963 there were 581 communes. See also the special issue of the *International Social Science Journal* (1961).

[3] On elections see Riddell (1968, pp. 58–9); Milivojevic (1965, pp. 16–20); *The Economist*, 15 April and 24 May 1969; and under earlier electoral regulations Hammand (1955).

[4] For a Yugoslav view see Jovanovic (1960). See also Kolaja (1965, pp. 29–34).

Perhaps their major function is educational, both educating workers to play their part in management, and in adult education generally; the Yugoslav unions have 'developed educational and cultural functions in recent years which are more comprehensive than those of any working class body known to the authors' (Singleton and Topham, 1963, p. 21). The power of the Unions over elections to the Workers' Councils has been curtailed (see below) and most of their other powers inside the enterprise are shared with other bodies and Kolaja found that the Union in the factories that he visited was dependent on the Council because of financial factors.[1]

Apart from these indirect channels, the obvious way for the League to make its influence felt is through the election of League members to the Workers' Councils. The proportion of Workers' Council members who are also League members varies widely, but it is often very high in an individual enterprise. Singleton and Topham cite an average of 35%; in the two factories visited by Kolaja it was 70% and just under 50% respectively, and a Yugoslav survey gave a range from 8% to 65%.[2] It may be that such large proportions of League members will not be elected as time goes on because of the change in election procedures in 1964. Originally, a list of candidates could be nominated by 10% of the workers or by the Union branch—usually this meant that the latter provided the lists. Now, candidates can be nominated by any worker and two seconders at a special meeting of the collective. There is competition for places; in the Split shipyard visited by Stephen, for example, there were 76 candidates for 35 places in 1967. The election is by secret ballot and is conducted by a special committee set up by the Council; a high proportion of workers vote, Stephen gives figures of 87% in 1966 and 91.2% in 1967.[3] One obstacle in the way of control by the League is the rapid rotation of Council members, office being for two years, with half replaced each year.[4]

From his investigations, Kolaja (1965, p. 63) concluded that the League

---

[1] Kolaja (1965, p. 34–35). A discussion of the role of Trade Unions in a demo-cratised industrial authority structure cannot be entered into here. Suffice it to say that the important function of the protection of the interests of individual workers qua workers would still remain, whatever the composition of management.

[2] Singleton and Topham (1963, p. 10); Kolaja (1965, p. 16, Table 1); cited I.L.O. (1962, p. 33).

[3] Stephen (1967, pp. 9–10). Blumberg (1968) says that the collective has to vote to approve the nomination (p. 200). For elections under the earlier system see Singleton and Topham (1963, p. 9).

[4] Blumberg (1968, p. 198) says that now no member may serve two consecutive terms. Riddell (1968, p. 66) gives figures for those elected in 1962 which show a considerable degree of continuity.

'apparently was not a frequent initiator, but rather an observer and censor'. But perhaps the most interesting evidence comes from the questionnaire administered by the same author in factory B that he visited. Of 78 respondents asked, 'Who has the greatest influence in the enterprise?', only four put the League first, eleven put it second in influence and nine third, whereas 45 put the Workers' Council first, 25 the Director and two the Union (p. 34, Table 12). Any evaluation of the role of the League, since it can work through many different directions, is extremely difficult. Perhaps all that needs to be said for our purposes is that, although the League obviously cannot be ignored, it would be a mistake to assume that, therefore, the whole organisational structure of industry counted for nothing. At present other external factors may weigh equally as heavily on the individual Workers' Council—namely economic factors. The Council is subject to influence over its policies from the Economic Associations (associations of enterprises making similar products) and, most importantly, since the 1965 economic reforms the enterprise operates within a virtually free-market economy, each enterprise competing with all the rest; the banks, a major source of credit, are also now autonomous bodies operating on 'capitalist' lines so far as credit is concerned. How compatible this relationship between a free market and socialised enterprises will prove in the long run remains to be seen, but in general, so far as these external factors are considered, there seems no good reason to suppose that, at any rate some, Workers' Councils cannot control their own affairs: 'Despite some restrictive laws, some intervention by the government and some pressure from the party, the workers' councils and their elected managing boards are in fact responsible for the control of their own enterprises' (Neal and Fisk, 1966, p. 30).

Given, then, that it is worth looking in more detail at the operation of the Yugoslav worker's self-management system, some questions of general applicability to any system of industrial democracy can now be raised; questions mentioned earlier when possible interpretations of 'impossible' were considered, that concern the extent to which any part-time management body of 'ordinary workers' can really control full-time expert staff. We shall also consider how far the mass of workers take up the opportunities formally open to them and how far it is possible, under the Yugoslav system, for the individual directly to participate in decision making as the participatory theory of democracy argues that he should.

One question that is worth examining is what sort of decisions are taken by the Workers' Councils; is there any evidence that such a body of workers, coming together at intervals as managers, finds it difficult to deal with the most important technical problems? Formally, the Council has very broad decision-making powers. Apart from functions already referred to, it

approves production, wage and marketing policies and plans; rules of conduct; and reports submitted by the managing board; it decides how that part of the earnings which is left to the disposal of the enterprise is to be distributed ... In general, the workers' council is entitled to be concerned with every problem of the enterprise. It is also the highest authority in the enterprise to which persons can appeal (Kolaja, 1965, p. 6).

The I.L.O. (1962) Report states that the workers' management bodies 'are directly responsible for some of the duties that elsewhere fall to top management and the senior and medium level executives—as regards a host of detailed decisions as well as policy matters' (p. 163). There is some information available as to how the Councils spend their time. Kolaja analysed the subjects discussed by the Workers' Councils in the factories that he visited (as recorded in the minutes from 1957 to 1959) and divided them into three categories. The first, the 'production-financial' (production planning, wages, purchase and sale of machines), corresponds roughly to our higher management level category; the other two, 'organisational-maintenance' and 'individual applications' (for leave and complaints, etc.) fit broadly into the lower management level. In both factories the Workers' Councils spent the greatest proportion of their time on matters falling into the first category.[1] The topics to which the Councils have devoted most attention have shown an interesting evolution over time. A content analysis of the minutes of seven enterprises, over a period of ten years, has shown that, over that period, the amount of time devoted to the most important, higher management, topics has increased, while that spent on other matters has decreased. The author argued that this indicated that the Workers' Council members had learned to deal with matters that transcended their immediate environment—or, as Riddell puts it, that they are 'slowly "catching up with the system" '.[2] This does provide some interesting support for the argument of the theorists of participatory democracy about the wider educative effect of participation, that it widens interests and outlook and develops the more practical capacities for political participation.[3]

[1] Kolaja (1965, p. 24, Table 6). Stephen found the same pattern in the Split shipyard (1967, p. 17). See also the list of agendas of 6,000 councils in Blumberg (1968, pp. 205–6) and the list of debates and decisions at the Rade Koncar enterprise in Kmetic (1967, pp. 27–8).

[2] From account in Kolaja, p. 23. Riddell (1968, p. 68).

[3] Sturmthal has suggested that this evolution merely reflects legal changes. Although the legal framework has changed, the powers of the Councils have always been extensive; the point is that they now seem more willing and able to exercise them. Sturmthal (1964, p. 109).

In one sense, because Councils are taking decisions of this nature, the possibility of a democratic authority structure in industry has been demonstrated; the 'government' is elected into office by the whole collective, is accountable to the electorate and replaceable by them. On the other hand the question remains of the role of the professional 'experts' in the enterprise; does the Workers' Council function as a rubber stamp for decisions that are effectively made elsewhere? The role of the Director is clearly important here, both formally and informally. The reduction of his term of office to four years means that the scope for the exercise of outright 'omnipotence' is reduced but he does, as already shown, have wide formal powers. Stephen (1967, p. 35) notes that in the shipyard he visited there was a provision in the 'statut' (constitution) that prevented the Council from changing a decision of the Director on the execution of policy decisions; their only recourse was to involve the Commune or dismiss the Director. How common such a provision is is not known. Certainly, in the past there have been many cases of Directors exceeding their powers and the Yugoslav press has given publicity to these.[1] Again it would seem that the position has now improved but, in this case, as in all others, it is difficult to generalise because of the wide differences in conditions in different parts of Yugoslavia. It would be far easier for a Director so-minded to 'take over' an enterprise in, say, Macedonia, where he would probably be dealing with an illeducated, industrially inexperienced workforce, than in the more industrially sophisticated Republic of Slovenia. Whatever the position regarding overt 'omnipotence' observations of Workers' Councils meetings indicate that the influence exercised by the Director and the Collegium and other 'experts' is considerable. Most suggestions appear to come from the Director and the Collegium and these are rarely rejected and they also seem to do most of the talking. This applies particularly when the more important and technical topics are discussed (e.g. production plans); it is only when lower level matters are discussed— particularly the issue of the allocation of the housing that Yugoslav enterprises provide for workers—that the rank and file Council members participate to any extent, or take notes, and it is on these issues that really vigorous debate occurs. The pattern was similar in the enterprise visited by Stephen where the labour force was fairly highly educated and skilled (though at the meeting he attended some of the higher level topics had been discussed previously).[2] On the other hand, one account does say that in the case of at

---

[1] See Ward (1957) and Tochitch (1964).

[2] Stephen (1967, pp. 38–41). Accounts of Workers Council meetings can be found in Riddell (1968, pp. 66–7) and Kolaja (1965, pp. 45–50 and 19–21, Table 4). In the factory visited by the former the workers were of low skill status; in those visited

least one enterprise 'Council and Economic Unit meetings attended were marked by very frequent voting, not normally unanimous, and many important decisions were taken which amended the proposals of the Director, Chairman and sub-committees' and the I.L.O. Report mentions a similar instance.[1]

Even allowing for some examples of active and effective participation on the part of the rank and file members of some Workers' Councils, the more general picture of the weight of influence exercised by the Director and other expert staff does highlight what looks, on the face of it, an almost insoluble dilemma for a democratic and participatory system in industry. If the maximum number of workers are to have the chance to hold management office and if the educative effect of participation is also to be maximised, then a short time in office on a part-time basis is necessary; but if Workers' Council members are effectively to discuss higher policy matters with their expert staff, then the opposite would seem to be required. In a relatively undeveloped country like Yugoslavia the dimensions of this dilemma are accentuated, but too far reaching implications should not be drawn from it. If this is what makes industrial democracy 'impossible' then, since a similar problem is faced by any elected democratic body (in local government for example), political democracy is impossible too—and the theorists who claim that industrial democracy is impossible do not wish to say that. The real question is the area in which a solution is to be sought to this dilemma in the industrial context; what means are available to Workers' Council members to enable them competently to evaluate and initiate plans and policies? One answer, of course, is experience; here the point made in the last chapter on the basis of the evidence of higher level partial participation is relevant. Participation at the higher level needs to be linked to opportunities for participation at the lower level as well. That is to say, just as participation in the workplace acts as a 'training ground' for participation in the wider political sphere, so experience of decision making at the lower management level can act as valuable training for participation in higher level decision making. The role of the economic units in Yugoslavia is vital in this respect. Secondly, we have seen that a necessary condition for participation is that the requisite information is available, and a lot more could be done in this direction in Yugoslavia. In general, information is made available to the workers in Yugoslav enterprises, ' "the principle of publicity" is probably unique, in most cases providing more information to employees in

by Kolaja a high proportion of the workers were women, though he does not seem to realise that this is significant for participation.

[1] Singleton and Topham (1963, p. 23), I.L.O. (1962, p. 236).

Yugoslavia than is supplied to their counterparts in Britain, or the United States, or in the Soviet Union'.[1] But, although one report says that in several enterprises Council and economic unit meetings 'were serviced with extensive documentation of the items on the agenda' this is not the case everywhere.[2] Although, as Sturmthal (1964, p. 189) points out, few managers in orthodox industrial systems take technical decisions by themselves, so that it is absurd to expect Council members to do so either, the latter still need the necessary 'countervailing' information to evaluate the suggestions of others. Here the Trade Unions could play a valuable role by obtaining and providing the Councils with this information, they could act as a kind of research department, or, as one Yugoslav discussion suggests, the Council could hire its own experts to do this kind of work.[3] Until solutions on the lines indicated here have been tried out the question of how far it is possible to reach a satisfactory solution to this dilemma must remain unanswered. Nevertheless, there is no good reason for supposing that its existence renders democratisation of industrial authority structures impossible.

We shall now turn to the question of the extent of the involvement of the mass of the workers in the workers' self-management system in Yugoslavia. The first point that must be made is that a remarkable number of persons have already held office; between 1950 and the early 1960s over a million individuals had served on Workers' Councils and Managing Boards, about a quarter of the industrial labour force.[4] Obviously, a large proportion of these must be 'ordinary' workers, but it should be noted that there is an ambiguity in the term 'Workers' Council' that few discussions of industrial democracy or workers' control do anything to resolve. The definition of a 'worker' is usually left open, and it is not stated whether 'workers' means only those who are manual or low status workers or whether the term includes workers 'by both hand and brain', i.e. all the employees in a particular enterprise. The implication of 'workers'' self-management or 'workers'' control is that lower status workers will be in a majority on the management bodies (which, as they form a majority of the labour force is acceptable enough), but there is no reason to confine 'workers'' self-management solely to this category of employee when democracy implies universal suffrage and that all should participate. In Yugoslavia the division between manual and white collar workers is

[1] Kolaja (1965, p. 76). See also I.L.O. (1962, p. 280).
[2] Singleton and Topham (1963, p. 24). See also Riddell, (1968, p. 66).
[3] Bilandzic (1967) and Dragicevic (1966).
[4] Blumberg (1968, p. 215). In 1960 the total labour force was 9m. of whom 5m. were agricultural workers. Auty (1965, p. 157.)

no longer officially recognised (Stephen, 1967, pp. 13) but it is not clear whether there are still provisions in force to ensure that managing bodies are composed predominantly of manual or production workers. Kolaja states that manual workers should be proportionately represented among candidates for the Council and that three-quarters of the Managing Board must be employed directly on production, but in the shipyard visited more recently by Stephen, they had no knowledge of the latter provision.[1] Whatever is the case here, it is difficult to see how, under any reasonably free nomination process, the provision as to candidates could be met, and there is no information on this. But, there is information on the composition of Workers' Councils and (in 1962) women tended to be under-represented, and skilled and highly skilled workers over-represented.[2] This last fact is illustrated by the Split shipyard, where, although from 1965 to 1967 the proportion of manual workers on the Workers' Council rose from 61.3% to 72.4%, in 1967 only 2.6% of these were semi-skilled and 3.9% unskilled.[3] The Split workers explained this low representation of the least skilled as due to generally low educational levels and the desire for the best men to hold office. It is difficult to see how these workers will increase their representation until educational levels rise, and until long-term experience has been gained of a participatory system, which would be expected to increase their psychological 'readiness' to participate.

Nevertheless, among the 'upper' working class there do seem to be fairly high rates of participation at the higher level. But this has to be set against a background where there is evidence of a more general lack of knowledge of, and interest in, the basic working of the system. In one of the factories that Kolaja visited he spoke to twenty-four people about the Workers' Council meeting, of whom ten knew nothing about it at all.[4] Riddell cites several Yugoslav surveys of general knowledge about the workers' self-management system and, although levels varied according to

[1] Kolaja (1965, pp. 7–8). Stephen (1967, p. 13). Blumberg (1968, p. 217) repeats the provision about the Managing Board.

[2] Riddell (1968, p. 66). This follows the same pattern as participation in political and social organisations in the West.

[3] Stephen (1967, p. 11 and App. 2:2:1). Of the white collar members only 3.9% were of elementary school level. (The white collar workers formed 13% of the total labour force.) Cf. Kolaja (1965, p. 17, Table 1).

[4] Kolaja (1965, p. 51). However, a former Chairman of the Council did remark that 'it is not the practice to report the workers council agenda to workers'. Kolaja goes further than his evidence warrants when he attributes the lack of participation in discussion of higher management questions on the part of rank and file Council members to lack of interest; in the absence of other evidence it could also be argued that it was lack of confidence or lack of sufficient information.

the type of worker and the type of factory, they tended to be low. In one factory 312 workers were asked who took the decisions in five areas of factory life and 105 answered none of the questions correctly and no workers got all five answers right. Another researcher commented that 'there is a striking fact that a comparatively large number of examinees possess no elementary knowledge and lack information on important social, economic and political problems'.[1] Riddell suggests that this lack of knowledge and interest is because 'in general the system has become too complicated for most of the workers who have to operate it'.[2] Certainly there are a host of regulations and they are frequently changed (and the system of income distribution is very complicated) but it is difficult to see how the actual organisational structure of workers'self-management could be any less complex and still allow for maximum participation, both direct and through representatives, at both higher and lower levels.

Unfortunately, most commentators virtually ignore lower level participation in the Yugoslav system so there is no means of telling whether levels of participation and interest are higher in that sphere (from the previous evidence on industrial participation one would expect that they might be).[3] This is unfortunate for another reason too. One of the problems raised in connection with the participatory theory of democracy was how far it would be possible to replicate the direct participatory model in the context of modern, large scale industry. The Yugoslav system does offer some ideas as to how this can be done. Firstly, a factor already referred to, the rapid rotation in office of the members of management bodies means that, over the course of a lifetime, every individual should have the opportunity to participate directly in decision making in that way at least once. Secondly, the Yugoslav system also offers every individual the opportunity to participate in decision making by the use of referenda in the enterprise on important topics. The I.L.O. Report mentions that these have mostly been on the question of the distribution of income, but in the Split shipyard a referendum was held on a Federal Government recommendation that the yard should form a consortium with three others. The vote was taken simultaneously in all four yards (under the jurisdiction of special committees) and the proposal did not go through as workers in one of the

---

[1] Cited Riddell (1968, pp. 62–3). See also Ward (1965).

[2] Riddell (1968, p. 64). One major difficulty in interpreting the Yugoslav evidence is what weight should be given to the gap that exists between official ideology and official practice; how far does this enter into the explanation of the low level of interest in the system?

[3] Blumberg (1968), for example, merely mentions the lower level developments in passing and makes no attempt to relate them to the information on participation presented earlier in his book.

yards voted against it.[1] The importance of lower level participation as a 'training ground' for participation in decision making has been mentioned before. Here the economic unit is very significant for it enables workers to participate in taking decisions of the same scope, for their own lower level collective, as higher management decisions are for the whole enterprise. According to one study 'the Yugoslavs regard the creation of Economic Units as one of the most significant developments of the last twenty years'.[2]

In most highly decentralised enterprises the relationship between the economic unit and the Workers' Council tends to take the form of a kind of collective contract and there have been instances of units discussing, and voting on, proposals to break away from the enterprise of which they are a part. They have wide functions which include the disposal of part of the internal funds of the enterprise, units sometimes borrowing from and lending to each other.[3] There is evidence that, at least in a few enterprises, workers do make use of the opportunities offered for lower level participation. Stephen notes that in the enterprise that he visited the less skilled and less educated workers had proportionately greater representation on the Departmental Councils and the I.L.O. Report describes a regular workshop meeting where 'comments and suggestions came from all sides . . . a third or more of the workers took part . . . and there was hardly any embarrassment due to verbal hesitancy . . . or difference in grades between the speakers' (I.L.O., 1962, p. 172).

One would not wish to claim that the system of workers' self-management in Yugoslavia provides a successful example of the democratisation of authority structures, or that the evidence presented here allows many firm conclusions to be drawn. Much more information is needed on many points; in particular, a comprehensive study is needed of the operation of the system in different types of enterprise in different areas of the country. Perhaps this will be made available in the future, for as Riddell (1968, p. 69) has pointed out, Yugoslavia 'provides a laboratory for research in the possibilities of decentralisation of control in modern large scale societies and its psychological effects. There are virtually no limitations—except those of language—to such research at the present period.' Despite these reservations, and the fact that the existence of the

---

[1] I.L.O. (1962, p. 172). Stephen (1967, pp. 43–4). The proposal was to be voted on again six months later.

[2] Singleton and Topham (1963, p. 17). These units were created originally to try to overcome the tendency of Councils to become aloof from the workers (p. 14).

[3] Singleton and Topham (1963, pp. 15–17) and (1963a). See also Kmetic (1967, pp. 20–6).

Communist League and the undeveloped nature of the Yugoslav economy makes direct comparisons with the West difficult, one conclusion that can be drawn is that the Yugoslav experience gives us no good reason to suppose that the democratisation of industrial authority structures is impossible, difficult and complicated though it may be.

This discussion of industrial democracy in Yugoslavia concludes the examination of the empirical evidence relevant to the arguments of the participatory theory of democracy. This evidence indicates that the general conclusion to be drawn so far as democratic theory is concerned is a clear one. The claim of the participatory theory of democracy that the necessary condition for the establishment of a democratic polity is a participatory society, is not a completely unrealistic one; whether or not the ideal of the earlier 'classical' theorists of participatory democracy can be realised remains very much an open and live question.

CHAPTER VI

Conclusions

Recent discussions of the theory of democracy have been obscured by the myth of the 'classical doctrine of democracy' propagated so successfully by Schumpeter. The failure to re-examine the notion of a 'classical' theory has prevented a proper understanding of the arguments of (some of) the earlier theorists of democracy about the central role of participation in the theory of democracy; prevented it even on the part of writers who wished to defend a participatory theory of democracy. This has meant that the prevailing academic orthodoxy on the subject, the contemporary theory of democracy, has not been subjected to substantive, rigorous criticism, nor has a really convincing case been presented for the retention of a participatory theory in the face of the facts of modern, large-scale political life.

The major contribution to democratic theory of those 'classical' theorists whom we have called the theorists of participatory democracy is to focus our attention on the interrelationship between individuals and the authority structures of institutions within which they interact. This is not to say that modern writers are completely unaware of this dimension; clearly this is not so, as much political sociology, especially that dealing with political socialisation, confirms, but the implications of the findings on socialisation for the contemporary theory of democracy have not been appreciated. The link between these findings, particularly those on the development of the sense of political efficacy in adults and children, and the notion of a 'democratic character' has been overlooked. Although many of the advocates of the contemporary theory of democracy argue that a certain type of character, or a set of psychological qualities or attitudes, is necessary for (stable) democracy—at least among a proportion of the population—they are far less clear on how this character could be developed or what the nature of its connection with the working of the 'democratic method' itself really is. While most do not support Schumpeter's declaration that the democratic method and the democratic character are unconnected, nor do they take much trouble to examine the nature of the postulated relationship. Even Almond and Verba, after clearly showing the connection between a participatory environment and the development of a sense of political efficacy, show no realisation of the significance of this in their final, theoretical chapter.

However, this failure is only part of a more general, and striking, feature of much recent writing on democratic theory. Despite the stress most modern political theorists lay on the empirical and scientific nature of their discipline they display, at least so far as democratic theory is concerned, a curious reluctance to look at the facts in a questioning spirit. That is, they seem reluctant to see whether or not a theoretical explanation can be offered of why the political facts are as they are; instead they have taken it for granted that one theory which could possibly have yielded an explanation had already been shown to be outmoded, and so concentrated on uncritically building a 'realistic' theory to fit the facts as revealed by political sociology.

The result of this one-sided procedure has been not only a democratic theory that has unrecognised normative implications, implications that set the existing Anglo-American political system as our democratic ideal, but it has also resulted in a 'democratic' theory that in many respects bears a strange resemblance to the anti-democratic arguments of the last century. No longer is democratic theory centred on the participation of 'the people', on the participation of the ordinary man, or the prime virtue of a democratic political system seen as the development of politically relevant and necessary qualities in the ordinary individual; in the contemporary theory of democracy it is the participation of the minority élite that is crucial and the non-participation of the apathetic, ordinary man lacking in the feeling of political efficacy, that is regarded as the main bulwark against instability. Apparently it has not occurred to recent theorists to wonder why there should be a positive correlation between apathy and low feelings of political efficacy and low socio-economic status. It would be more plausible to argue that the earlier democratic theorists were unrealistic in their notion of the 'democratic character' and in their claim that it was, given a certain institutional setting, open to every individual to develop in this direction, if the persons today who do not measure up to this standard were to be found in roughly equal proportions in all sections of the community. The fact that they are not should surely cause empirical political theorists to pause and ask why.

Once it is asked whether there might not be institutional factors that could provide an explanation for the facts about apathy as suggested in the participatory theory of democracy, then the argument from stability looks far less securely based. Most recent theorists have been content to accept Sartori's assurance that the inactivity of the ordinary man is 'nobody's fault' and to take the facts as given for the purpose of theory building.

Yet we have seen that the evidence supports the arguments of Rousseau, Mill and Cole that we do learn to participate by participating and that feelings of political efficacy are more likely to be developed in a participatory environment. Furthermore, the evidence indicates that experience of a participatory authority structure might also be effective in diminishing tendencies toward non-democratic attitudes in the individual. If those who come newly into the political arena have been previously 'educated' for it then their participation will pose no dangers to the stability of the system. Oddly enough, this evidence against the argument from stability should be welcomed by some writers defending the contemporary theory, for they occasionally remark that they deplore the low levels of political participation and interest that now obtain.

The argument from stability has only seemed as convincing as it has because the evidence relating to the psychological effects of participation has never been considered in relation to the issues of political, more specifically, democratic theory. Both sides in the current discussion of the role of participation in modern theory of democracy have grasped half of the theory of participatory democracy; the defenders of the earlier theorists have emphasised that their goal was the production of an educated, active citizenry and the theorists of contemporary democracy have pointed to the importance of the structure of authority in non-governmental spheres for political socialisation. But neither side has realised that the two aspects are connected or realised the significance of the empirical evidence for their arguments.

However, the socialisation aspect of the participatory theory of democracy is also capable of being absorbed into the general framework of the contemporary theory, providing the foundation for a more soundly based theory of stable democracy than those offered at present. The analysis of participation in the industrial context has made it clear that only a relatively minor modification of existing authority structures there may be necessary for the development of the sense of political efficacy. It is quite conceivable, given recent theories of management, that partial participation at the lower level may become widespread in well-run enterprises in the future because of the multiplicity of advantages it appears to bring for efficiency and the capacity of the enterprise to adapt to changing circumstances. Nevertheless, if the socialisation argument is compatible with either theory, the two theories of democracy remain in conflict over their most important aspect, over their respective definitions of a democratic polity. Is it solely the presence of competing leaders at national level for whom the electorate can periodically vote, or does it also require that a participatory society exist, a society so organised that every individual has the opportunity directly to participate in all political spheres? We have not, of course, set out to prove that it is one or the other; what we have been considering is whether the idea of a participatory society is as completely unrealistic as those writers contend who press for a revision of the participatory theory of democracy.

The notion of a participatory society requires that the scope of the term 'political' is extended to cover spheres outside national government. It has already been pointed out that many political theorists do argue for just such an extension. Unfortunately this wider definition, and more importantly its implications for political theory, are usually forgotten when these same theorists turn their attention to democratic theory. Recognition of industry as a political system in its own right at once removes many of the confused ideas that exist about democracy (and its relation to participation) in the industrial context. Its rules out the use of 'democratic' to describe a friendly approach by supervisors that ignores the authority structure within which this approach occurs, and it also rules out the argument that insists that industrial democracy already exists on the basis of a spurious comparison with national politics. There is very little in the empirical evidence on which to base the assertion that industrial democracy, full higher level participation, is impossible. On the other hand there is a great deal to suggest that there are many difficulties and complexities involved; more than are indicated for example in the early writings of G. D. H. Cole.

Although few firm conclusions can be drawn from the material on the system of workers' self-management in Yugoslavia, the fact that in an unfavourable setting for such an experiment it has worked at all, and worked to some degree, however small, as it is meant to in theory, is evidence that cannot be disregarded. The solutions suggested in the last chapter to some of the problems involved in establishing a system of industrial democracy, such as that of the dilemma between the control of 'experts' and provision for the maximum participation on the managing body, are tentative in the extreme; until we have an example of a system where 'countervailing information' is available to an elected managing body we have no means of knowing whether this might provide an acceptable answer (although perhaps the fact that the management will also be workers experienced in operating the establishment at shop floor level should not be underestimated where questions of expertise are concerned).

The major difficulty in a discussion of the empirical possibilities of democratising industrial authority structures is that we do not have sufficient information on a participatory system that contains opportunities for participation at both the higher and lower levels to test some of the arguments of the participatory theory of democracy satisfactorily. The importance of the lower level in the participatory process in industry is illustrated by evidence from both Britain and Yugoslavia. The lower level plays the same role *vis à vis* the enterprise as participation in industry generally does to the wider, national political sphere. The evidence suggests that the low existing level of demand for higher level participation in the workplace might, at least in part, be explained as an effect of the socialisation process which, both through the notion of his role-to-be at work gained by the ordinary boy and through the experiences of the individual inside the workplace, could lead to the idea of higher level participation being 'unavailable' for many workers. Thus, the possibility of lower level participation is crucial for the answer to the question of the number of workers who, in the long run, could be expected to take up the opportunities offered in a democratised system. In the absence of this vital training ground, even if higher level participation were introduced on a large scale, this would be unlikely by itself to elicit a large response from among rank and file workers (or therefore have much effect on the development of the sense of political efficacy). So whether the vast majority of workers would actively participate in a democratised industrial system as the theory of participatory democracy assumes that they would, must at this stage remain a question largely of conjecture, although the demand for lower level participation suggests that, providing that opportunities for this were available, more workers might ultimately do so than is thought possible by those most sceptical about industrial democracy.

Today, the question of economic efficiency is bound to loom very large in any discussion of the issues involved in democratising industrial authority structures; in particular how far the economic equality implied in a system of industrial democracy would be compatible with efficiency. Economic equality is often dismissed as of little relevance to democracy yet once industry is recognised as a political system in its own right then it is clear that a substantive measure of economic equality is necessary. If inequalities in decision-making power are abolished the case for other forms of economic inequality becomes correspondingly weaker. The example of the Scott Bader Commonwealth indicates that a large measure of job security for the ordinary worker is not incompatible with efficiency and the considerable inequalities that exist in security of tenure of employment (and in the various fringe benefits that are associated with that security) would seem to be the most salient aspect of economic inequality in modern terms. (Certainly without such security the individual independence that Rousseau valued so highly is impossible.) The Commonwealth also operates within a narrow salary range but it is difficult to say very much on the extent to which equalisation of incomes—what most people would naturally think of first when economic equality is mentioned—would ultimately be compatible with economic efficiency, the whole question of 'incentives', for instance, is a much disputed one, or indeed, to estimate how great a degree of equality in this sense is required for effective participation. Nor would it be very fruitful to speculate how elected managing bodies might weigh up the factors involved in income distribution within the enterprise, but the Yugoslav experience, as time goes on, may offer some useful guidance on this score. In general the evidence shows no obvious, serious impediments to economic efficiency that would call into question the whole idea of industrial democracy.[1] In fact much of the evidence on lower level participation gives support to Cole's view that a participatory system would release reserves of energy and initiative in the ordinary worker and so increase efficiency. But even if some inefficiency did result from the introduction of democratic decision making in industry whether or not this would provide a conclusive argument for its abandonment would depend on the weight given to the other results that could also be expected to accrue, the human results which the theorists of participatory democracy regarded as of primary significance.

We have considered the possibility of establishing a participatory society with respect to one area only, that of industry, but because industry occupies a vitally important place in the theory of participatory democracy, that is sufficient to establish the validity, or otherwise of the notion of a participatory society. The analysis of the concept of participation presented here can be applied to other spheres, although the empirical questions raised by the extension of participation to areas other than industry cannot be considered. Nevertheless, it might be useful to indicate briefly some of the possibilities in this direction.

To begin, as it were, at the beginning, with the family. Modern theories of child-rearing—notably those of Dr Spock—have helped to influence family life, especially among middle-class families, in a more democratic direction than before. But if the general trend is toward participation the educative effects arising from this may be nullified if the later experiences

---

[1] Little mention has been made of the question of ownership of industry under a participatory system as this would have taken us too far from our main theme. As shown by the examples of higher level partial participation in Britain there is a far wider choice of alternatives available than is suggested by the dichotomy usually posed between 'capitalism' and 'total nationalisation'. An interesting recent discussion on ownership can be found in Derrick and Phipps (1969, pp. 1–35).

of the individual do not work in the same direction. The most urgent demands for more participation in recent years have come from the students and clearly these demands are very relevant to our general argument. With regard to the introduction of a participatory system in institutions of higher education, it is sufficient to note here that if the arguments for giving the young worker the opportunity to participate in the workplace are convincing then there is a good case for giving his contemporary, the student, similar opportunities; both are the mature citizens of the future. One person whom the opportunities for participation in industry would pass by is the full-time housewife. She might find opportunities to participate at the local government level, especially if these opportunities included the field of housing, particularly public housing. The problems of running large housing developments would seem to give wide scope to residents for participation in decision making and the psychological effects of such participation might prove extremely valuable in this context. There is little point in drawing up a catalogue of possible areas of participation but these examples do give an indication of how a move might be made toward a participatory society.

A defender of the contemporary theory of democracy might object at this point that although the idea of a participatory society might not be completely unrealistic, this does not affect his definition of democracy. Even though authority structures in industry, and perhaps other areas, were democratised this would have little effect on the role of the individual; this would still be confined, our objector might argue, to a choice between competing leaders or representatives. The paradigm of direct participation would have no application even in a participatory society. A similar point was raised in the discussion of the system of workers' self-management in Yugoslavia, and it was clear that, within the industrial context, this objection is misplaced. Where a participatory industrial system allowed both higher and lower level participation then there would be scope for the individual directly to participate in a wide range of decisions while at the same time being part of a representative system; the one does not preclude the other.

If this is the case where the alternative areas of participation are concerned, there is an obvious sense in which the objection is valid at the level of the national political system. In an electorate of, say, thirty-five millions the role of the individual must consist almost entirely of choosing representatives; even where he could cast a vote in a referendum his influence over the outcome would be infinitesimally small. Unless the size of national political units were drastically reduced then that piece of reality is not open to change. In another sense, however, this objection misses the point because it rests on a lack of appreciation of the importance of the participatory theory of democracy for modern, large scale, industrialised societies. In the first place it is only if the individual has the opportunity directly to participate in decision making and choose representatives in the alternative areas that, under modern conditions, he can hope to have any real control over the course of his life or the development of the environment in which he lives. Of course, it is true that exactly the same decisions are not made, for example, in the workplace as in the House of Commons or the Cabinet, but one may agree with Schumpeter and his followers in this respect at least: that it is doubtful if the average citizen will ever be as interested in all the decisions made at national level as he would in those made nearer home. But having said that, the important point is, secondly, that the opportunity to participate in the alternative areas would mean that one piece of reality would have changed, namely the context within which all political activity was carried on. The argument of the participatory theory of democracy is that participation in the alternative areas would enable the individual better to appreciate the connection between the public and the private spheres. The ordinary man might still be more interested in things nearer home, but the existence of a participatory society would mean that he was better able to assess the performance of representatives at the national level, better equipped to take decisions of national scope when the opportunity arose to do so, and better able to weigh up the impact of decisions taken by national representatives on his own life and immediate surroundings. In the context of a participatory society the significance of his vote to the individual would have changed; as well as being a private individual he would have multiple opportunities to become an educated, public citizen.

It is this ideal, an ideal with a long history in political thought, that has become lost from view in the contemporary theory of democracy. Not surprisingly perhaps when for some recent writers such a wide-ranging democratic ideal is regarded as 'dangerous', and they recommend that we pitch our standards of what might be achieved in democratic political life only marginally above what already exists. The claim that the Anglo-American political system tackles difficult questions with distinction looks rather less plausible since, for example, the events in the American cities of the late 1960s or the discovery in Britain that in the midst of affluence many citizens are not only poor but also homeless, than it may have done in the late 1950s and early 1960s, but such a statement could have only seemed a 'realistic' description then because questions were never asked about certain features of the system or certain aspects of the data collected, despite the much emphasised empirical basis of the new theory. In sum, the contemporary theory of democracy represents a considerable failure of the political and sociological imagination on the part of recent theorists of democracy.

When the problem of participation and its role in democratic theory is placed in a wider context than that provided by the contemporary theory of democracy, and the relevant empirical material is related to the theoretical issues, it becomes clear that neither the demands for more participation, nor the theory of participatory democracy itself, are based, as is so frequently claimed, on dangerous illusions or on an outmoded and unrealistic theoretical foundation. We can still have a modern, viable theory of democracy which retains the notion of participation at its heart.

Bibliography

(Together with works cited in the text, the bibliography contains some further sources
to which reference was made)

Alford, R. F. (1964), *Party and Society*, John Murray, London.
Almond, G. A., and Verba, S. (1965), *The Civic Culture*, Little Brown & Co.,
Boston.
Anderson, N. (1961), *Work and Leisure*, Routledge & Kegan Paul, London.
Argyris, C. (1957), *Personality and Organisation*, Harper Bros., New York.
—— (1964), *Integrating the Individual and the Organisation*, Wiley, New York.
Auty, P. (1965), *Yugoslavia*, Thames & Hudson, London.
Bachrach, P. (1967), *The Theory of Democratic Elitism: A Critique*, Little, Brown &
Co., Boston.
Banks, J. A. (1963), *Industrial Participation*, Liverpool University Press.
Barratt Brown, M. (1960), 'Yugoslavia Revisited,' *New Left Review*, No. 1, pp. 39–43.
——(1960a), 'Workers' Control in a Planned Economy', *New Left Review*, No. 2,
pp. 28–31.
Barry, B. M. (1964), 'The Public Interest', *Proceedings of the Aristotelian Society*, supp.
vol. 38, pp. 1–18.
Bay, C. (1965), 'Politics and Pseudo-politics', *American Political Science Review*,
vol. LIX, No. 2, pp. 39-51.
Bell, D. (1960), 'Work and its Discontents' in *The End of Ideology*, Free Press, New
York.
Bendix, R. (1956), *Work and Authority in Industry*, Wiley, New York.
Bendix, R., & Fisher, L. H. (1962), 'The Perspectives of Elton Mayo' in Etzioni, A.
(ed.) *Complex Organisations*, Holt, Rinehart, New York.
Bentham, J. (1843), *Works*, Bowring, J. (ed.) Tait, Edinburgh.
Berelson, B. R. (1952), 'Democratic Theory and Public Opinion', *Public Opinion
Quarterly*, vol. 16, No. 3, pp. 313–30.
Berelson, B. R., Lazarsfeld, P. F., & McPhee, W. N. (1954), *Voting*, University of
Chicago Press.
Berlin, I. (1958), *Two Concepts of Liberty*, Oxford University Press.
Bilandzic, D. (1967), 'Workers' Management of Factories', *Socialist Thought and
Practice*, No. 28, pp. 30–47.
Blau, P. M., & Scott, W. R. (1963), *Formal Organisations*, Routledge & Kegan Paul,
London.
Blauner, R. (1960), 'Work Satisfaction and Industrial Trends in Modern Society' in
Galenson, W., and Lipset, S. M. (eds.) *Labour and Trade Unionism*, Wiley, New
York.
——(1964), *Freedom and Alienation*, University of Chicago Press.

Blum, F. H. (1968), *Work and Community*, Routledge & Kegan Paul, London.

Blumberg, P. (1968), *Industrial Democracy: The Sociology of Participation*, Constable, London.

Boston, R. (1968), 'What Leisure?' *New Society*, 28 Dec.

Brown, W. (1960), *Exploration in Management*, Heinemann, London.

Burns, J. H. (1957), 'J. S. Mill and Democracy', *Political Studies*, vol. v, No. 1, pp. 158–75, and No. 2, pp. 281–94.

Campbell, A., Gurin G., & Miller, W. (1954), *The Voter Decides*, Row, Peterson, Illinois.

Carey, A. (1967), 'The Hawthorne Studies: A Radical Critique', *American Sociological Review*, vol. 32, No. 3, pp. 403–16.

Carpenter, L. P. (1966), *G. D. H. Cole: An Intellectual Biography*, Unpublished Ph.D. Thesis, Harvard.

Chamberlain, N. W. (1958), *Labour*, McGraw Hill, New York.

—— (1963), 'The Union Challenge to Management Control', *Industrial and Labour Relations Review*, vol. 16, No. 2., pp. 184–91.

Chandler, M. K. (1964), *Management Rights and Union Interests*, McGraw Hill, New York.

Chinoy, E. (1955), *Automobile Workers and the American Dream*, Doubleday, New York.

Clegg, H. A. (1960), *A New Approach to Industrial Democracy*, Blackwell, Oxford.

Coates, K. (ed.) (1968), *Can the Workers Run Industry*, Sphere Books, London.

Coates, K., & Topham, A. (1968), *Industrial Democracy in Great Britain*, Macgibbon & Kee Ltd., London.

Cobban, A. (1964), *Rousseau and the Modern State*, Geo. Allen & Unwin, London.

Coch, L., & French, J. R. P. (1948), 'Overcoming Resistance to Change, *Human Relations*, vol. 1, No. 4, pp. 512–32.

Cole, G. D. H. (1913), *The World of Labour*, G. Bell & Sons, London,

—— (1915), 'Conflicting Social Obligations', *Proceedings of the Aristotelian Society*, vol. xv, pp. 140–59.

—— (1918), *Labour in the Commonwealth*, Headley Bros., London.

—— (1919), *Self-government in Industry*, G. Bell & Sons, London.

—— (1920), *Social Theory*, Methuen, London.

—— (1920a), *Guild Socialism Restated*, Leonard Parsons, London.

—— (1920b), *Chaos and Order in Industry*, Methuen, London.

'Commune in Yugoslavia, the' (1961) Special Issue, *International Social Science Journal*, vol. xiii, No. 3.

Cotgrove, S. (1967), *The Science of Society*, Geo. Allen & Unwin, London.

Dahl, R. A. (1956), *Preface to Democratic Theory*, University of Chicago Press.

—— (1956a), 'Hierarchy, Democracy and Bargaining in Politics and Economics' in Eulau, H., Eldersveld, S., and Janowitz M. (eds.) *Political Behaviour*, Free Press, Glencoe.

—— (1963), *Modern Political Analysis*, Prentice-Hall, New Jersey.

—— (1966), 'Further Reflections on the "Elitist Theory of Democracy" ', *American Political Science Review*, vol. lx, No. 2, pp. 296–306.

Davis, L. (1964), 'The Cost of Realism: Contemporary Restatements of Democracy', *Western Political Quarterly*, vol. xvii, pp. 37–46.

Day, R. C., & Hamblin, R. L. (1964), 'Some Effects of Close and Punitive Styles of Supervision', *American Journal of Sociology*, vol. lxix, No. 5, pp. 499–510.

Deleon, A. (1959), 'Workers' Management', *Annals of Collective Economy*, vol. XXX, pp. 143–67.

Derrick, P., & Phipps, J. F. (1969), *Co-ownership, Co-operation and Control*, Longmans, London.

'Draft Theses on the Future Development and Reorganisation of the League of Communists of Yugoslavia' (1967), *Socialist Thought and Practice*, No. 26.

Duncan, G., & Lukes, S. (1963), 'The New Democracy', *Political Studies*, vol. XI, No. 2, pp. 156–77.

Durkheim, E. (1960), *Montesquieu and Rousseau*, University of Michigan Press.

Easton, D., & Dennis, J. (1967), 'The Child's Acquisition of Regime Norms; Political Efficacy', *American Political Science Review*, vol. LXI, No. 1, pp. 25–38.

—— (1969), *Children in the Political System: Origins of Political Legitimacy*. McGraw Hill, New York.

Eckstein, H. (1966), 'A Theory of Stable Democracy', App. B of *Division and Cohesion in Democracy*, Princeton University Press.

Exley, R. (1968), 'Paternalist, Genius, Visionary, Dictator, Industrial Guru?', *Help*, No. 1, pp. 25–9.

Farganis, J., & Rousseas, S. W. (1963), 'American Politics and the End of Ideology', *British Journal of Sociology*, vol, 14, pp. 347–62.

Flanders, A., Pomeranz, R., & Woodward, J. (1968), *Experiment in Industrial Democracy*, Faber & Faber, London.

French, J. R. P., Israel, J., & Aas, D. (1960), 'An experiment in Participation in a Norwegian Factory', *Human Relations*, vol. 13, No. 1, pp. 3–19.

Friedmann, G. (1961), *The Anatomy of Work*, Heinemann, London.

Glass, S. T. (1966), *The Responsible Society*, Longmans, London.

Goldschmidt, M. L. (1966), 'Democratic Theory and Contemporary Political Science', *Western Political Quarterly*, vol. XIX, No. 3, pp. 5–12.

Goldthorpe, J. H., Lockwood, D., Bechhofer, F., & Platt, J. (1968), *The Affluent Worker: Industrial Attitudes and Behaviour*, Cambridge University Press.

Greenstein, F. I. (1965), *Children and Politics*, Yale University Press.

Guest, R. H. (1962), 'A controlled Experiment in Job Enlargement' in Walker, C. R. (ed.) *Modern Technology and Civilisation*, McGraw Hill, New York.

Hadley, R. (1965), *Common Ownership in Action* and *Common Ownership and Management*, Scott Bader & Co. Ltd.

Halliday, R. J. (1968), 'Some Recent Interpretations of J. S. Mill', *Philosophy*, vol. XLIII, No. 163, pp. 1–17.

Hamburger, J. (1962), 'James Mill on Universal Suffrage and the Middle Class', *Journal of Politics*, vol. 24, No. 1, pp. 167–90.

—— (1965), *Intellectuals in Politics*, Yale University Press.

Hammond, T. (1955), 'Yugoslav Elections: Democracy in Small Doses', *Political Science Quarterly*, vol. LXX, No. 1, pp. 57–74.

Harrison, R. (1957), 'The Congress of Workers' Councils, Yugoslavia', *New Reasoner*, vol. 1, No. 2, pp. 99–102.

Herbst, P. G. (1962), *Autonomous Group Functioning*, Tavistock, London.

Herzberg, F., Manser, B., & Snyderman, B. (1959), *The Motivation to Work*, Wiley, New York.

Herzberg, F. (1968), *Work and the Nature of Man*, Staple Press, London.

Holter, H. (1965), 'Attitudes towards Employee Participation in Company Decision Making Processes', *Human Relations*, vol. 18, No. 4, pp. 297–319.

Horvat, B., & Rascovic, V. (1959), 'Workers' self-government in Yugoslavia', *Journal of Political Economy*, vol. LXVII, No. 2, pp. 194–8.

Hyman, H. H. (1954), 'The Value Systems of Different Classes' in Bendix R., and Lipset, S. M. (eds.) *Class, Status and Power*, 1st ed., Routledge & Kegan Paul.

—— (1959), *Political Socialisation*, Free Press, Glencoe.

International Labour Office (1962), *Workers' Management in Yugoslavia*, Geneva.

Jaques, E. (1951), *The Changing Culture of a Factory*, Tavistock, London.

—— (1968), *Employee Participation and Managerial Authority*, London.

Jaros, D., Hirsch, H., & Fleron, F. J. (1968), 'The Malevolent Leader: Political Socialisation in an American Sub-Culture', *American Political Science Review*, vol. LXII, No. 2, pp. 564–75.

Jarvie, M. (1968), *An Experiment in Industrial Democracy: The Rowen Engineering Co. Ltd*. Unpublished paper, Edinburgh University.

Jovanovic, Z. (1966), 'Trades Unions and Workers' Management', *Socialist Thought and Practice*, No. 22, pp. 66–85.

Kariel, H. S. (1956), 'Democracy Unlimited: Kurt Lewin's Field Theory', *American Journal of Sociology*, vol. LXII, No. 3, pp. 280–9.

Kelly, J. (1968), *Is Scientific Management Possible?* Faber & Faber, London.

Klein, J. (1965), *Samples from English Culture*, 2 vols., Routledge & Kegan Paul.

Kmetic, M. (1967), *Self-management in the Enterprise*, Belgrade.

Knupfer, G. (1954), 'Portrait of the Underdog', in Bendix, R, and Lipset, S. M. (eds.), *Class, Status and Power*, Routledge & Kegan Paul, London.

Kolaja, J. (1965). *Workers' Councils: The Yugoslav Experience*, Tavistock, London.

Lammers, C. J. (1967), 'Power and Participation in Decision-making in Forma Organisations', *American Journal of Sociology*, vol. 73, No. 2, pp. 201–16.

Lane, R. E. (1959), *Political Life*, Free Press, New York.

Laswell, H. D., & Kaplan, A. (1950), *Power and Society*, Yale University Press.

Likert, R. (1961), *New Patterns of management*, McGraw Hill, New York.

Lipset, S. M. (1960), *Political Man*, Heinemann, London.

Lipsitz, D. (1964), 'Work Life and Political Attitudes', *American Political Science Review*, vol. LVIII, No. 4, pp. 951–62.

Loucks, W. N. (1958), 'Workers' Self-government in Yugoslav Industry', *World Politics*, vol. XI, No. 1, pp. 68–82.

Lupton, T. (1963), *On the Shop Floor*, Pergamon, Oxford.

—— (1966) *Management and the Social Sciences*, Hutchinson, London.

McFarlane, B. (1966), 'Yugoslavia's Crossroads' in Merlin Press, *Socialist Register*, London.

McGregor, D. (1960), *The Human Side of Enterprise*, McGraw Hill, New York.

Mayo, H. B. (1960), *Introduction to Democratic Theory*, Oxford University Press.

Melman, S. (1958) *Decision Making and Productivity*, Blackwell, Oxford.

Merton, R. (1962) 'Bureaucratic Structure and Personality', in *Social Theory and Social Structure*, Free Press, Glencoe.

Milbrath, L. W. (1965), *Political participation*, Rand McNally, Chicago.

Milivojevic, D. (1965), *The Yugoslav Commune*, Belgrade.

Mill, J. (1937), *An Essay on Government*, Cambridge University Press.

Mill, J. S. (1910), *Representative Government*, Everyman ed.

—— (1924), *Autobiography*, World's Classics ed.

—— (1963), *Essays on Politics and Culture*, Himmelfarb G. (ed.), New York.

—— (1965), *Collected Works*, Robson, J. M. (ed.), University of Toronto Press.

Mills, C. W. (1963), 'The Unity of Work and Leisure', in Horowitz, I. L. (ed.) *Power, Politics and People*, Oxford University Press.

Morris Jones, W. H. (1954), 'In Defence of Apathy', *Political Studies*, vol. II, pp. 25–37.

Morse, N. C., & Weiss, R. S. (1955), 'The Function and Meaning of Work and the Job', *American Sociological Review*, vol. 20, No. 21, pp. 191–8.

Mussen, P. H., & Wyszynski, A. B. (1952), 'Personality and Political Participation', *Human Relations*, vol. V, No. 1, pp. 65–82.

Neal, F. W. (1958), *Titoism in Action*, University of California Press.

Neal, F. W., & Fisk, W. M. (1966), 'Yugoslavia—Towards a Market Socialism', *Problems of Communism*, vol. XV, No. 6, pp. 28–37.

O'Donnell, C. (1952), 'The Source of Managerial Authority', *Political Science Quarterly*, vol. 67, pp. 573–88.

Orren, K., & Peterson, P. (1967), 'Presidential Assassination: A case study in the Dynamics of Political Socialisation', *Journal of Politics*. vol. 29, No. 2, pp. 388–404.

Ostergaard, G. (1961), 'Approaches to Industrial Democracy', *Anarchy*, No. 2, pp. 36–46.

Partridge, P. H. (1963), 'Some Notes on the Concept of Power,' *Political Studies*, vol. XI, pp. 107–25.

Plamenatz, J. (1958), 'Electoral Studies and Democratic Theory', *Political Studies*, vol. VI, pp. 1–9.

—— (1963), *Man and Society*, Longmans, London.

Pospielovsky, D. (1968), 'Dogmas under Attack: A Traveller's Report', *Problems of Communism*, vol. XVII, No. 2, pp. 41–7.

Pribicevic, B. (1959), *The Shop Stewards Movement and Workers' Control*, Blackwell, Oxford.

Pym, D. (1968), 'Individual Growth and Strategies of Trust' in Pym, D. (ed.), *Industrial Society*, Penguin Books.

Rhenman, E. (1968), *Industrial Democracy and Industrial Management*, Tavistock, London.

Rice, A. K. (1958), *Productivity and Social Organisation: The Ahmedabad Experiment*, Tavistock, London.

Riddell, D. (1968), 'Social Self-government: The Background of Theory and Practice in Yugoslav Socialism', *British Journal of Sociology*, vol. XIX, No. 1, pp. 47–75.

Riesman, D. (1950), *The Lonely Crowd*, Yale University Press.

—— (1964), 'Leisure, and Work in Post Industrial Society' in *Abundance for What?* Chatto & Windus, London.

Robson, J. M. (1968), *The Improvement of Mankind*, University of Toronto Press.

Rokkan, S., & Campbell, A. (1960), 'Norway and the United States of America', in 'Citizen Participation in Political Life', Special Issue, *International Social Science Journal*, vol. XII, No. 1.

Rosenburg, M. (1954), 'Determinants of Political Apathy', *Public Opinion Quarterly*, vol. XVIII, No. 4, pp. 349–66.

—— (1962), 'Self-esteem and Concern with Public Affairs', *Public Opinion Quarterly*, vol. XXVI, No. 2, pp. 201–11.

Rousseau, J. J. (1911), *Emile*, Everyman ed.

—— (1913), *A Discourse on Political Economy*, Everyman ed.

—— (1953), *Rousseau: Political Writings*, Watkins, F. (trans.), Nelson, London.

—— (1965), *The Political Writings*, Vaughan, C. E. (ed.), Blackwell, Oxford.
—— (1968), *The Social Contract*, Cranston, M. (trans.), Penguin Books.
Rowen Factories (1967), *Donors News Bulletin*, No. 5.
Rubinstein, A. Z. (1968), 'Reforms, Non-alignment and Pluralism', *Problems of Communism*, vol. XVII, No. 2, pp. 31–41.
Russell, B. (1938), *Power*, George Allen & Unwin, London.
Sartori, G. (1962), *Democratic Theory*, Wayne State University Press, Detroit.
Sawtell, R. (1968), *Sharing our Industrial Future?* The Industrial Society, London.
Schumpeter, J. A. (1943), *Capitalism, Socialism and Democracy*, Geo. Allen & Unwin, London.
Scott Bader (1961), Scott Bader & Co. Ltd.
Scott Bader Commonwealth (n.d.), Scott Bader & Co. Ltd.
Seliger, M. (1968), *The Liberal Politics of John Locke*, Geo. Allen & Unwin, London.
Shklar, J. (1964), 'Rousseau's Images of Authority', *American Political Science Review*, vol. LVIII, No. 4, pp. 919–32.
Singleton, F., & Topham, T. (1963), *Workers' Control in Yugoslavia*, Fabian Research Series, 233, Fabian Society, London.
—— (1963a), 'Yugoslav Workers' Control: The Latest Phase', *New Left Review*, No. 18, pp. 73–84.
Smith, A. (1880), *An inquiry into the Nature and Causes of the Wealth of Nations*, 2nd. ed., Clarendon Press, Oxford.
Stephen, F. H. (1967), *Management Structure and Industrial Relations in a Yugoslav Shipyard*, Unpublished paper, Glasgow University.
Stephens, L. (1962), 'A Case for Job Enlargement', *New Society*, 11 Oct.
Sturmthal, A. (1964), *Workers' Councils*, Harvard University Press.
Sugarman, B. (1968), 'The Phoenix Unit: Alliance Against Illness', *New Society*, 6 June.
Talmon, J. L. (1952), *The Origins of Totalitarian Democracy*, Secker & Warburg, London.
Tannenbaum, A. S. (1957), 'Personality Change as a Result of an Experimental Change of Environmental Conditions', *Journal of Abnormal and Social Psychology*, vol. 55, pp. 404–6.
Taylor, C. (1967), 'Neutrality in Political Science' in Laslett, P., and Runciman, W. G. (eds.) *Philosophy, Politics and Society*, 3rd series, Blackwell, Oxford.
Tochitch, D. (1964), 'Some Aspects of Workers' Management', *Review*, No. 4, pp. 235–52.
Trist, E. L., & Bamforth, K. W. (1951), 'Some Social and Psychological Consequences of the Longwall Method of Coal-getting', *Human Relations*, vol. IV, No. 1, pp. 3–38.
Trist, E. J., & Emery, F. E. (1962), 'Socio-technical Systems', in Walker, C. R. (ed.) *Modern Technology and Civilisation*, McGraw Hill, New York.
Trist, E. L., Higgin, G. W., Murray, H., & Pollock, A. B. (1963), *Organisational Choice*, Tavistock, London.
Turner, H. A. (1963), *The Trend of Strikes*, Leeds University Press.
Verba, S. (1961), *Small Groups and Political Behaviour*, Princeton University Press.
Walker, C. R. (ed.) (1962), *Modern Technology and Civilisation*, McGraw Hill, New York.
Walker, C. R., & Guest, R. H. (1952), *The Man on the Assembly Line*, Harvard University Press.

BIBLIOGRAPHY

Walker, J. L. (1966), 'A Critique of the Elitist Theory of Democracy', *American Political Science Review*, vol. LX, No. 2, pp. 285–95.

Ward, B. (1957), 'Workers' Management in Yugoslavia', *Journal of Political Economy*, vol. LXV, No. 5, pp. 373–86.

—— (1965), 'The Nationalised Firm in Yugoslavia', *American Economic Review*, vol. LV, No. 2, pp. 65–74.

Webb, J. (1962), 'The Sociology of a School', *British Journal of Sociology*, vol. XIII, pp. 264–72.

White, R., & Lippitt, R. (1960), 'Leader Behaviour and Member Behaviour in Three Social Climates', in Cartwright, D., and Zander, A. (eds.) *Group Dynamics*, 2nd. ed., Tavistock, London.

Wolin, S. (1961), *Politics and Vision*, Geo. Allen & Unwin, London,

Woodward, J. (1958), *Management and Technology*, H.M.S.O.

Woodward, J. L., & Roper, E. (1950), 'Political Activity of American Citizens', *American Political Science Review*, vol. XLIV, No. 4, pp. 872–85.

Wright, R. (1961), 'The Gang System in Coventry', *Anarchy*, No. 2, pp. 47–52.

Young, S. 'The Question of Managerial Prerogatives', *Industrial and Labour Relations Review*, vol. 16, No. 2, pp. 240–53.

Zweig, F. (1961), *The Worker in an Affluent Society*, Heinemann, London.

Index

Aas, D., 68, 70
Alford, R. F., 49 n.
Almond, G. A., 15 n., 46–50, 74, 103
Argyris, C., 52–3, 54 n.
authoritarianism: Eckstein on need for, 13, 74–5, 83
authoritarian personality, 3, 10, 64, 105
authority structures: and individual attitudes, 22, 24–5, 29–31, 42–3, 47–66, 73–4, 103, 105; democratisation of in industry, 86–102, 106–7; Eckstein on congruency of, 12–13
Auty, P., 88 n., 92 n., 98 n.

Bachrach, P., 4 n., 14, 15 n., 16, 17 n., 21 n., 84 n.
Bader, E., 80, 82
Barry, B. M., 24 n.
Bay, C., 15 n.
Bell, D., 55, 69 n.
Bentham, J., 17, 31, 36; criticised by J. S. Mill, 28–9; on function of participation, 19–20; on role of electorate, 18–19
Berelson, B. R., 5, 8, 15, 42; on deficiencies of 'classical' theory, 6–7
Berlin, I., 27 n.
Bilandzic, D., 98 n.
Blauner, R., 51–2, 54, 55, 56, 57, 59, 62
Blum, F. H., 79 n., 80 n., 81, 82, 87 n.
Blumberg, P., 56 n., 58–9, 63, 64, 65, 66, 72 n., 73, 89 n., 90 n., 91 n., 93 n., 95 n., 98 n., 99 n., 100 n.
Boston, R., 56 n.
Brown, W., 75 n.
Burke, E., 20 n.
Burns, J. H., 28 n.

Campbell, A., 46
Carpenter, L. P., 40 n.

Carey, A., 65 n.
Chamberlain, N. W., 75 n.
Chandler, M. K., 75 n.
Chinoy, E., 54 n.
'classical' theory of democracy, 3, 42, 102, 103; a myth, 17–21; Berelson on, 6–7; Dahl on, 8; Eckstein on, 11 n.; ideals of, 16, 21; Schumpeter on, 4, 17–18
Clegg, H. A., 71–2
Coates, K., 71 n.
Coch, L., 59 n.
Cole, G. D. H., 21, 27, 45, 60, 83, 88, 105, 106, 108; his plan for guild socialism, 40–1; his principle of function, 37; his theory of associations, 36–7; on economic efficiency, 40, 108; on economic equality, 39–40; on educative function of participation, 38; on encroaching control, 60; on other functions of participation, 39 n.; on political equality, 38–9; on representation, 37, 40
commune, in Yugoslavia, 90 n., 92
Communist League, of Yugoslavia, 89, 91–4, 106
composite longwall mining, 61
contemporary theory of democracy, 13–14, 20, 45, 82, 103–5, 109–11; contrasted to participatory theory, 43; criticisms of, 15; not value-free, 15–16
control: and participation, 25–7, 56–8, 71 n., 110; encroaching, see encroaching control; of 'experts', 86, 87–8, 96–8, 106; of leaders: Cole on, 40; Dahl on, 8; in contemporary theory of democracy, 14; Rousseau on, 26; Schumpeter on, 5
conventional longwall mining, 60–1
Cotgrove, S., 49

Kaplan, A., 69
Kariel, H. S., 71 n.
Kelly, J., 75 n., 76, 77
Klein, J., 49 n.
Kmetic, M., 89 n., 90 n., 95 n., 101 n.
Knupfer, G., 50
Kolaja, J., 92, 93, 95, 96 n., 98 n., 99

Labour Party, 86 n.
Lammers, C. J., 67
Laswell, H. D., 69
leisure: and development of political efficacy, 54–6
Lewin, K., 63, 64, 71
Likert, R., 62, 65, 67, 69
Lippitt, R., 63 n.
Lipset, S. M., 15 n.
Lipsitz, D., 52 n., 54 n.
Locke, J., 20
Lukes, S., 5 n., 15 n., 16, 17 n., 29 n.
Lupton, T., 66 n.

Madison, J., 9
Marx, K., 35
Maslow, A. H., 64
Mayo, H. B., 15 n.
McGregor, D., 65, 67
Melman, S., 61–2
Merton, R., 53 n.
Michels, R., 2, 86
Milbrath, L. W., 15 n., 20, 46 n., 79 n.
Mill, J., 17, 31; on function of participation, 19–20; on role of electorate, 18–19
Mill, J. S., 17, 20, 21, 27, 36, 38, 45, 47, 61 n., 74, 105; ambiguity in his theory of participation, 32–3; criticisms of Bentham, 28–9; his notion of participation, 32; on educative function of participation, 29–31; on industry, 33–4; on natural state of society, 31–2; on other functions of participation, 33; on participation in local government, 30–1; on political equality, 32
Mills, C. W., 55 n.
Milivojevic, D., 92 n.
Morris, W., 35
Morris Jones, W. H., 15 n.
Morrison, H., 86 n.
Mosca, G., 2

Neal, F. W., 91 n., 94

O'Donnell, C., 75 n.
Orren, K., 48 n.
Ostergaard, G., 72

participation: and development of sense of political efficacy, 47–9, 51–66, 73–4; educative function, 24–5, 29–31, 38, 42, 74, 95, 110; in Cole's theory, 36–8; in contemporary theory of democracy, 14; in participatory theory of democracy, 43; J. S. Mill's notion of, 32–3; protective function, 14, 19–20, 24; Rousseau's notion of, 24–5; subsidiary functions, 27, 33, 39 n., 63–4; see also, industrial participation, participatory society, political efficacy, political socialisation
participation hypothesis, the, 63
participatory society, 20, 21, 35, 37, 43, 44, 83, 87 n., 105–6, 108, 109; Cole's plan for, 40–1, 60
participatory theory of democracy, 20–1, 35, 42–4, 53, 60, 63–4, 83, 109–10; and political socialisation, 45–50, 73–4, 103–5
Partridge, P. H., 69
Phipps, J. F., 87, 108 n.
Plamenatz, J., 15 n., 24
political, the, 35, 43–4, 83–4, 106
political competence, see political efficacy
political efficacy: and democratic theory, 103–5; and lower level partial participation, 73–4; defined, 46; development of, in children, 48–9; through leisure, 54–6; through local participation, 47; through organisational participation, 47; through participation in family and school, 49; through participation in the workplace, 49, 51–66, 73–4; not sufficient for active participation, 74
political equality, see equality, political
political socialisation: and democratic theory, 103–5, 110; importance of workplace in, 49, 51–3; in contemporary theory of democracy, 14; in participatory theory of democracy, 42–3; of children, 47–9; see also, political efficacy, social training

polyarchy, 8–10
power: and influence, 69–70
Pribicevic, B., 40 n.

representative government, theorists of, 20
Rhenman, E., 92 n.
Rice, A. K., 61 n.
Riddell, D., 91 n., 92 n., 93 n., 95, 96 n., 98 n., 99, 100, 101
Riesman, D., 55
Robson, J. M., 30 n., 31 n., 33
Rokkan, S., 49 n.
Rousseas, S. W., 15 n.
Rousseau, J.-J., 17, 18, 20, 21, 30, 32, 33, 35, 36, 37, 39, 56, 63, 74, 105, 107; his notion of participation, 24; on being one's own master, 26, 63–4; on economic equality, 22–3; on educative function of participation, 24–5; on freedom, 25–6; on groups, 24; on other functions of participation, 27, 63–4; on political equality, 23–4
Rowen Engineering Company, 87–8
Rubinstein, A. Z., 91 n.
Russell, B., 75 n.

Sartori, G., 5, 16, 104; on reasons for apathy, 11; on role of democratic theory, 10
Sawtell, R., 67, 71 n., 87 n.
Schumpeter, J., 3, 6, 8, 16, 19, 20, 22 n., 24 n., 29, 40, 103, 110; his realistic definition of democracy, 4; on 'classical' theory of democracy, 4, 17–18; on control of leaders, 5; on necessary conditions for democracy, 4–5
Scott Bader Commonwealth, 79–83, 107
Seliger, M., 20 n.
Shklar, J., 25 n.
Singleton, F., 89 n., 90 n., 93, 97 n., 98 n., 101 n.
Skeffington Report, 1
small group experiments, 63–4
Smith, A., 51 n.
Spock, Dr, 108
social training: Dahl on, 9–10, 45; *see also* political socialisation

Stephen, F. H., 90 n., 93, 95 n., 96, 99, 101
Stephens, L., 58, 69 n.
Sturmthal, A., 95 n., 98
Sugarman, B., 73 n.
supervisory styles, 63, 65

Talmon, J. L., 27 n.
Tannenbaum, A. S., 64
Taylor, C., 15
Taylor, F., 64
Tochitch, D., 96 n.
Tocqueville, A. de, 30
Topham, T., 89 n., 90 n., 93, 97 n., 98 n., 101 n.
totalitarianism, 2, 11, 16, 26 n.
Trist, E. L., 60 n., 61
Turner, H. A., 56

Verba, S., 15 n., 46–50, 63, 64, 69, 74, 103

Walker, C. R., 57 n., 58 n.
Walker, J. L., 15
Ward, B., 96 n., 100 n.
Webb, J., 49 n.
Weimar Republic, 2
White, R., 63 n.
Wolin, S., 19 n.
workers' self-management, *see* Yugoslavia
Wright, R., 62

Young, S., 75 n.
Yugoslavia: workers' councils in, and control of 'experts', 97–8; and the Commune, 92; and the Trade Unions, 92–3; discussions in, 95; formal powers of, 95; role of Communist League in, 91–4; role of Director in, 96–7; structure of, 89–90; workers' self-management in, and direct democracy, 100–1; economic performance under, 90–1; economic units in, 89, 101; workers' involvement in, 98–101

Zweig, F., 57 n.